56688 9 50H

D1475893

Virgil's
THE
AENEID

AND
THE GEORGICS
THE ECLOGUES

JULIA WOLFE LOOMIS
DEPARTMENT OF GREEK AND LATIN
COLUMBIA UNIVERSITY

MONARCH
PRESS

MONARCH PRESS

Copyright © 1964 by
SIMON & SCHUSTER

All rights reserved. No part of this book may be
reproduced in any form without permission in
writing from the publisher.

Published by
MONARCH PRESS
a Simon & Schuster division of
Gulf & Western Corporation
Simon & Schuster Building
1230 Avenue of the Americas
New York, N.Y. 10020

MONARCH PRESS and colophon are trademarks
of Simon & Schuster, registered in the U.S. Patent
and Trademark Office.

Standard Book Number: 0-671-00509-X

Library of Congress Catalog Card Number: 65-7176

Printed in the United States of America

CONTENTS

Brief Genealogy Showing Relationship of JULIUS CAESAR and AUGUSTUS

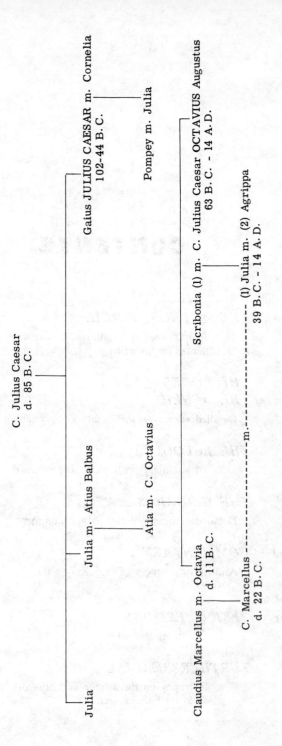

LIFE OF VIRGIL

Publius Vergilius Maro was born in a small country village, Andes, near Mantua on October 15, 70 B.C. Tradition says his mother's name was Magia Polla, the daughter of a certain man of property, Magius, for whom Virgil's father worked at one time. From careful study of his poems and from references in early biographers, we learn that he was the son of a middle class farmer, received some education at the nearby city of Cremona, and possibly further education at Milan. He took his "graduate courses" in Rome and Naples, where the usual curriculum included rhetoric, philosophy, science and literature. He spent most of his adult life in Naples, but he incorporates into his poetry the most beautiful scenes from all the regions where he had lived. We have no definite knowledge of the events in his life until the year 42 B.C.

The battle of Philippi took place in October of that year between Julius Caesar's heirs, Antony and Octavius, and Brutus and Cassius (the old-guard faction, responsible for Caesar's assassination in 44 B.C.) To compensate the veterans of their victorious armies, Octavius and Antony confiscated land in the north of Italy. This was the very region where Virgil's father's farm was located. Through the influence of the governor of the territory, Asinius Pollio, Virgil was able to prevail upon Octavius to spare his father's farm. It is to this Pollio that he subsequently dedicated his first mature work, The Bucolics, or as they are more commonly called, The Eclogues (from the Greek word meaning "select poems"). These are short pieces about the joys and sorrows of idealized shepherds. There is evidence that Virgil lived both in Rome and in various country villas while he was composing the Eclogues. These were published around 37 B.C.

The next ten years of his life were occupied in writing his great work on farming, The Georgics. It is probable that they were first published about 30 B.C., and then revised in 26 B.C. (see introduction to Georgics for details). During much of this period the idea of writing a great epic was in the back of Virgil's mind. After the completion of the Georgics, he spent the rest of his life on the Aeneid. It was not yet ready for publication when in 19 B.C. he decided to take a trip to Greece and Asia Minor. He intended to devote three years there to the careful revision of the work. But while he was in Athens, he met Augustus who was returning to Rome to straighten affairs that had become out of hand during his four years absence from the capital. He persuaded Virgil to return with him. At Megara in Greece, Virgil caught a fever, and grew more and more ill during the voyage across the Adriatic Sea. He died on September 21, 19 B.C., shortly after his arrival in the port of Brundisium. He was not quite fifty-one years old.

Much has been written about Virgil's character and temperament. These works are opinions based on what each writer has felt most keenly through his own reading of the poems. The best way to understand Virgil is to read his works over and over again. He was a humble man who respected and admired the men in prominent positions who were his patrons: Pollio, Varus, Gallus, Maecenas, and finally the emporer Augustus himself. He had a burning sense of the importance of the mission of Rome. The beauty and history of his native land moved him deeply. Most important of all, he was filled with those yearnings which impel all great men: the desire for peace, the search after the nature of the divine and for inner contentment, and the longing to express one's beliefs in a form worthy of the greatest of his predecessors.

Genealogy of the HOUSE OF TROY

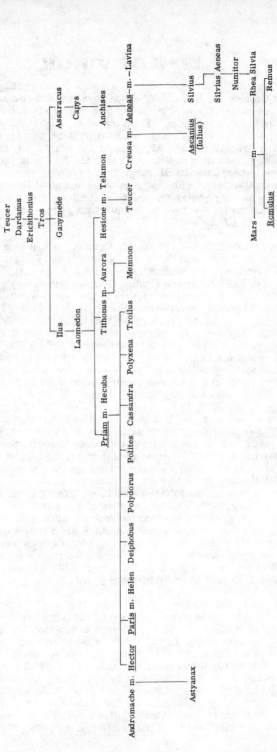

TABLE OF GODS AND GODDESSES

GREEK NAME	ROMAN NAME	FUNCTION
Zeus	Jupiter	King of the gods
Hera	Juno	Queen of the gods, goddess of marriage and childbirth
Pallas Athena	Minerva	Goddess of wisdom
Poseidon	Neptune	King of the sea, patron of horses
Aphrodite	Venus	Goddess of love
Eros	Cupid	Son of Venus, god of love
Ares	Mars	God of war
Artemis	Diana	Goddess of the moon, of the hunt, and of chastity
Phoebus Apollo	Apollo	Sun-God, god of healing, patron of the arts
Demeter	Ceres	Goddess of seed-time and Harvest
Persephone	Proserpina	Queen of the underworld, daughter of Ceres
Hades	Pluto	King of the underworld
Kronos	Saturn	Father of Jupiter, Pluto, Neptune, ruler of the old order of gods
Hermes	Mercury	Messenger of the gods
Dionysus	Bacchus	God of wine
Hephaestus	Vulcan	God of fire

DATES

B.C.			
70	Birth of Virgil and Gallus	42	Battle of Philippi
65	Birth of Horace	37	Publication of Eclogues
63	Birth of Octavius	31	Battle of Actium
59	Consulship of Caesar	27	Octavius assumes title of Augustus
55	Traditional death of Lucretius	26	Death of Gallus
48	Battle of Pharsalia	22	Death of Marcellus
48-44	Caesar supreme	19	Death of Virgil
44	Caesar's assassination	A.D.	
		14	Death of Augustus

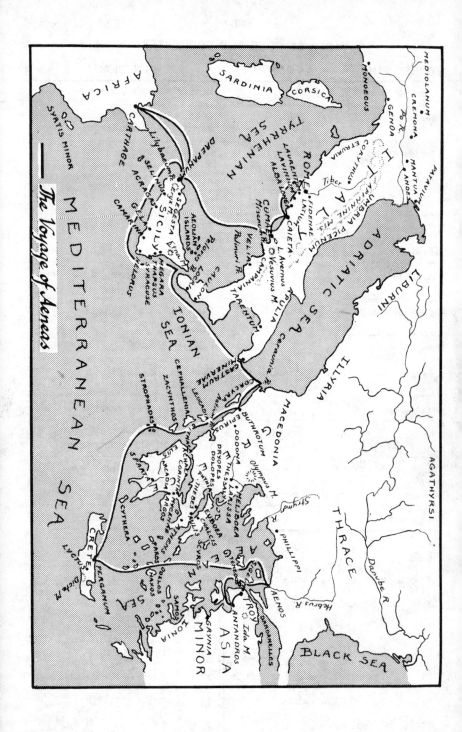

The Voyage of Aeneas

THE AENEID

INTRODUCTION   The Aeneid is an epic. Webster's dictionary defines epic as follows: "A long narrative poem about the deeds of a traditional or historical hero or heroes of high station, such as the Iliad or Odyssey, with a background of warfare and the supernatural, a dignified style, and certain formal characteristics of structure (beginning in the middle of the story, catalogue passages, invocation of the muse, etc)." It is important to keep these points in mind in reading the Aeneid, but if we expect an exciting fulfillment of the first part of the definition, we shall be disappointed. The actual plot of the poem is weak.   In fact, if the gods and goddesses did not interfere all the time, there would barely be any plot at all. Aeneas, the son of the goddess of love, Venus, and a prince of Troy, Anchises, escapes from the sack of Troy with a loyal group of fugitives. Their destination is Italy. They have a few insignificant adventures, mostly in the form of warnings about what to avoid.

They almost reach Italy but the queen of the gods, Juno, intervenes. She is angry that they have made the trip so easily, and sends a storm which drives them to Africa and the city of Carthage. There the hero meets the queen, Dido, makes love to her, and leaves her, because the king of the gods, Jupiter, tells him he must. He has a destiny, to found Rome. Aeneas obeys and sails away. Dido leaps on her burning funeral pyre, and dies.

The hero, after a short stay in Sicily and a trip to the underworld, eventually arrives in Italy. There the natives are friendly until Juno stirs them up.   The fortunes of the ensuing war ebb and flow, but finally Aeneas kills the enemy's champion. There the story ends. The tale of the deeds of Aeneas, however, is not the main reason for the poem. Virgil wrote the Aeneid because he was obsessed with the idea of Rome's mission to the world. He wanted to create a work of art to rival the Iliad and Odyssey of Homer. He was a complex poet, and took as a skeleton the myth of Aeneas (which had existed in various forms for centuries) to convey the thoughts burning within him.

It is impossible not to compare the Aeneid with Homer's two epics. In such a comparison, however, the Aeneid always seems to suffer. This is because so many people think that Virgil's poem tried to be a combination of Homer's two, and failed.   The hero, Aeneas, doesn't seem to be made of flesh and blood, as are Achilles and Hector, the great warriors of the Iliad. When we read Homer, we are right there with the leaders of both sides, Greek and Trojan.   There is tremendous excitement. In the Odyssey, we accompany the clever scoundrel, Odysseus, on his adventures which equal the thrill of the Arabian Nights. However insurmountable the obstacle, Odysseus always manages to come out on top. Aeneas, on the other hand, has really very few true adventures. He sails, he lands somewhere, and talks to someone who warns him about what will happen next. Except for his affair with Dido and his trip to the underworld, his so-called adventures are quite uneventful.

In Homer, the characters are men; in Virgil they are symbols first, and men only second. This brings us to the important point. The two poets can be compared, as they have been for centuries, and always will be. But if we come to a conclusion which says that the Iliad is full of life and vigor, and the Aeneid is slow and dull, we have totally missed the difference in the aims of the two poets. Homer's main purpose is to tell a story. Virgil's purpose is to show symbolically how Rome achieved her greatness. Both portray human character, but Virgil starts from the symbol and molds his characters to fit the symbol. Aeneas is symbolic both of the progress of Rome in history, and of Augustus' rise to the position of leader of the civilized world. Homer's heroes are examples of certain types of human character, but he did not consciously intend to make them symbols. Aeneas always acts fully aware of time past and time future, but hardly at all concerned with the present. Achilles and Hector, although a sense of tragedy hangs over them, are basically creatures of the present. We could go on enumerating differences. The point is that because Virgil built his poem on a Greek model, using his own original conception of the symbolic aspects of human character and history, he was able to create a work which not only added hitherto unknown depths to the power of the Latin language, but which appeals to us now as it did to the men of the Renaissance, and will to future generations.

We cannot leave the discussion of Virgil's models without a brief mention of two of the earlier Latin poets who wrote epics. Both their works exist only in such small fragments that a thorough comparison is not possible. The elder of these, Naevius, fought in the first war with Carthage (the First Punic War, 264-241 B.C.). When it was over he lived at Rome and wrote the story of the war as an epic poem. Its title was the Punic War. In the introduction he discussed the mythical origins of Rome and Carthage, Aeneas' escape from Troy, the storm at sea, Jupiter's promise to Venus concerning Rome's future greatness, Aeneas' visit to Dido's city, and the settlement of the Trojans in Latium. All of these elements are found in Virgil's poem. The rest of Naevius' work, however, dealt with the historical events of the Punic War itself.

The other early Roman writer of epic who influenced Virgil was Ennius (236-169 B.C.). Born in a small town, he served in the army, and eventually moved to Rome where he wrote poetry and plays. His epic of eighteen books was, like that of Naevius, based on history. It was called the Annals. The first book covered the period from the death of the king of Troy, Priam, to the deification of the founder of Rome, Romulus. Virgil's twelve books cover only part of Ennius' first one. The rest of the Annals was what we would call a history book about Rome. It could hardly be called a unified poem. Unfortunately we possess too little of these poets' works to discuss with any degree of certainty their similarities to Virgil. The great difference between Virgil and his Latin predecessors was that he transcended history by writing of myth, and thus gave his poem a universal application. Greek or Roman, he challenges all his models in the Aeneid.

Virgil probably commenced work on the poem before he completed the Georgics. In the introduction to the third Georgic he says that he is going to write an epic. Indeed, it was the great goal of his life. Perhaps he had composed a rough draft as early as 30 B.C. We have no way of knowing. But the rest of his life was occupied with the Aeneid. In 19 B.C. it was almost finished except for a few half lines and some passages he had not gone over. That year he planned a trip to Greece and Asia Minor where he intended to spend at least three years going over the work. He went as far as Athens where the emperor was staying on the last leg of his journey back to Rome. He persuaded Virgil to return to Italy with him. Before leaving Greece, Virgil fell ill. He lived only long enough to reach the Italian port of Brundisium. His dying wish was to have the poem destroyed because of its poetic imperfections, and inconsistencies in the plot. But Augustus ordered it published after Virgil's two literary executors had gone over it.

The poem consists of twelve books, the longest of which is 952 lines, the shortest, 705. The subjects of the books are as follows:

I: The invocation to the muse, the causes of Juno's anger, the wreck of Aeneas' fleet, and the arrival in Carthage where Aeneas meets Dido.

II: Aeneas' tale of the fall of Troy and his escape.

III: The tale of the adventures of the exiles on their voyage from Troy to Italy.

IV: The tragic love of Dido for Aeneas, the Trojan's departure from Africa, and Dido's death.

V: Festival of sports held in Sicily in honor of Aeneas' dead father, Anchises.

VI: Aeneas' visit to the prophetic Sibyl and his journey to the underworld.

VII: Landing in Latium in Italy, and Juno's rousing the native prince, Turnus, to fight the Trojans.

VIII: Aeneas' expedition up the Tiber to find allies in the war, his learning early Italian myths, and the start of the fighting while he is absent.

IX: Expedition of two Trojans, Nisus and Euryalus, to break through the enemy's camp and inform Aeneas of Turnus' attack, the burning of the Trojan ships, and Turnus' magnificent fighting.

X: The unproductive council of the gods, the return of Aeneas, and his search for Turnus whom Juno spirits away from the field of battle.

XI: Truce for both sides to bury their dead, the breaking of the treaty, and the renewal of fighting where the Trojans drive the enemy back within its own city walls.

XII: Encounter of the two champions, Aeneas and Turnus, and Turnus' death.

Virgil manipulates these characters and events to portray symbolically the whole history of Rome. He sees this history as an incorporation of three separate concepts:

1. the presence of the divine in men because of their ability to think and create lawful society;
2. the idea of heroes with a destiny;
3. the world of historical people and events.

At times he treats these concepts individually; at times they are woven together. It is this unique three-way vision of the poet, this ability to see human character and history symbolically, that enables Virgil to be ranked among the greatest poets of the world.

BOOK I

The opening eleven lines of the Aeneid are a brief introduction in the epic tradition of Homer. Virgil announces that his story will concern the deeds and sufferings of a man (Aeneas) who is driven from Troy by destiny and a sense of divine duty. Aeneas' task is to found the city of Rome, but he is being kept from fulfilling this duty by the anger of the queen of the gods, Juno, the wife of Jupiter. Virgil appeals to the goddess of inspiration, the muse of poetry, to tell him the reasons for Juno's anger and to aid him in his great task of writing the poem.

> **COMMENT:** Aeneas was a fugitive from the Trojan War and a native of Troy, which was located in north-eastern Asia Minor. He is now sailing somewhere in the Mediterranean with twenty ships on his way to Italy. Virgil mentions Troy in the introduction not only to recall the ancient legend that Rome's ancestors came from Asia Minor, but also to indicate his relation as a Roman poet to the Greek Homer, whose great epic, the Iliad, tells of the adventures of the Greek warriors in their attempts to capture Troy. But Aeneas is more than a hero such as Odysseus (whose wanderings after the Trojan War are told in Homer's Odyssey). Aeneas has a divine mission, symbolic of Virgil's conception of the divine mission of Rome. Aeneas' task is to found a city which will eventually be called Rome. Rome's mission is to govern the world with order and justice. This symbolic relation of Aeneas and Rome must be kept in mind through the whole poem, for otherwise Aeneas may seem to be a rather insipid sort of person and not at all like a hero. The poet alludes to the three steps in the founding of Rome when he mentions Latium, where Aeneas built the first city, Lavinium; Alba Longa, which was founded by Aeneas' son, Ascenius; and thirdly Rome, built by Romulus, a distant descendant of Ascanius.

The next seventy lines or so discuss the reasons for Juno's anger and her plan to get rid of the Trojans by having their ships destroyed in a storm. Juno is the patron diety of Carthage, a city located on the coast of Africa. It was founded by settlers from two Phoenician cities in Syria, Tyre and Sidon. (Historically this event took place around 800 B.C.) Juno wants Carthage to rule the world (instead of Rome) and decides to try and keep the Trojans from reaching their destined shore, Italy. If Rome is never founded, Juno thinks, then Carthage will have no rival; she has heard that if the city of Rome is built, descendants from that city will one day destroy her beloved Carthage. This is the first reason for her anger at the Trojans.

The second reason for her ire is that she was not selected when the Trojan prince, Paris, made the famous judgment as to which goddess was the most beautiful. The other two goddesses were Venus, the goddess of beauty and love, and Minerva, the goddess of wisdom. Venus was chosen the beauty-queen because she bribed Paris with a gift of the fairest mortal in the world, Helen. This is called the "Judgment of Paris."

A third was that the Trojans were decended from Jupiter, who was her husband, and another woman, a mortal. The final reason for Juno's anger was that Ganymede, a member of the royal house of Troy, was selected as the cupbearer of the gods, replacing her daughter Hebe. After enumerating these reasons for Juno's wrath, Virgil gives the reader a glimpse of the Trojan fleet sailing just beyond Sicily. We then go back to Juno, who decides to call a halt to their happiness. She goes to the king of the winds, Aeolus, to ask him to let loose the storm winds which he keeps chained in a cave. Juno is brooding all the while that she, the wife of Jupiter, should be allowed to cause storms if Minerva (Pallas Athena in Greek), who was only one of Jupiter's daughters, could cause them. To persuade him, Juno offers Aeolus a beautiful nymph (Diaopea). Aeolus consents, and strikes the mountain cave. The winds come shrieking out.

> **COMMENT:** This passage is important because in it the reader meets the gods for the first time. To the poet Virgil, the function of the gods has two aspects: practical and symbolic. The practical aspect is that they serve to keep the story going by participating in the events. The symbolic aspect is that they serve to point up the various sides of human nature. Juno represents much that is bad: passion, anger, lack of control. On the other hand, Aeolus and Jupiter (whom we shall meet in the next passage) represent the control of the mind that leads to order. Virgil, and the whole Roman world of his time, was preoccupied with the idea of law and order because of the terrible period of disorder through which he had just lived: Italy had been plunged in Civil War for some eighty years preceeding Octavius; victory at Actium in 31 B.C. where he defeated Anthony and Cleopatra. The reader must keep in mind the contrast of emotion and reason, violence and order in the Aeneid.

NAMES AND PLACES

TIBER: the river in Italy on which Rome is situated.

SAMOS: a Greek island in the Aegean Sea where an ancient temple to Juno was located.

LIBYA: used to mean all of Africa under Carthaginian rule.

FATES: refers to the three goddesses who controlled the thread of human life: Clotho held the spindle, Lachesis drew the thread, Atropos cut it.

ARGOS: one of the most important cities in Greece to supply fighters to Troy in the Trojan War. It is emphasized here because Juno had a great temple there.

TEUCER: the mythical founder of Troy. Teucrian race is another way of saying Trojan, but it also indicates the Roman's reverence for their ancestors.

AJAX SON OF OILEUS: (not the famous Ajax, son of Telemon, who plays an important role in the Iliad). His fleet was destroyed by Pallas Athena when he was returning from Troy; he had violated the prophetess, Cassandra (Priam's daughter) before the altar of Athena.

AEOLIA: a small island northeast of Sicily. Referring to this island Virgil subtly reminds the reader of Homer's Odyssey. Odysseus, in his wanderings after the Trojan War, visited Aeolia. The king of the island, Aeolus, (as Homer tells the story) gave Odysseus a bag with all the storm winds tied up to insure favorable weather. After leaving, his companions, thinking it contained treasure, untied the bag. The ensuing storm brought on all Odysseus' troubles.

TYRRHENIAN SEA: lies southwest of Italy.

ILIUM: another name for Troy.

GODS: refers here to the household gods of the Romans, the Lares Penates. The Lares were the spirits of the dead who protected the home where they had lived. The Penates protected the food and material prosperity of the family. Images of the Lares and Penates were placed near the hearth, and at each meal offerings were made to them.

(LINES 81-156.) Aeolus now releases the shrieking winds from the cave, and the resulting storm causes the destruction of Aeneas' fleet. In the midst of the thunder, lightning, surging sea, and black sky, Aeneas cries out in despair, wishing that he had died with his friends before the walls of Troy and the eyes of his parents. That would have been a noble death compared to drowning. But the storm grows worse. The oars break, three ships run afoul on the rocks, one ship goes down before Aeneas' very eyes, and all of them seem to be foundering. At this point the sea-god, Neptune, becomes aware of what is going on. He is angered at Aeolus for causing a storm without asking his permission. With the aid of two lesser sea divinities, Cymothoë the sea nymph, and Triton the trumpeter, Neptune proceeds to undo the harm caused by Aeolus and his winds. The roaring ocean subsides and the remains of Aeneas' fleet make for the nearest shore (Africa). Virgil likens Neptune's calming of the storm to an orator who is able to sway and command huge crowds.

COMMENT: The preceeding passage is important because here Aeneas enters the story. From his words in the depths of the storm we learn something of his character. First we learn that Aeneas is burdened by a sorrowful and loving memory of Troy. Yet he derives a strength from this memory which eventually enables him to found a new city. The speech, in a sense, forshadows the development of Aeneas' character. Here Aeneas is only looking back to his past, but as the story unfolds we find Aeneas both looking back and looking to the future, and to the founding of Rome. The last step in his development occurs when he no longer looks back to Troy at all but is filled only with thoughts of Rome. The second thing we learn about Aeneas' character is his sense of filial devotion. This duty to and love of parents was a very important aspect of Roman life.

NAMES AND PLACES

SARPEDON: a son of Jupiter and a Trojan ally.

SIMOIS: a small river near Troy.

TRIDENT: a three-pronged spear, symbol of Neptune's power. Neptune was also the patron of horses and horseracing.

SIMILE: This word does not appear in the story but the comparison of Neptune with the orator is a simile. It is very important in the understanding of Virgil's art to notice how he uses these. Usually his similes are drawn from the natural or spiritual worlds. That is why this one is particularly interesting, for it seems to come from the Rome of Virgil's youth: in those strife-torn days when he was a boy, there were many orators who could sway the masses, such as the famous Cicero.

(LINES 157-222.) At long last Aeneas and his friends reach land, though they do not know that the harbor they have come to is in Africa quite close to Carthage. Their first concern is to get themselves dried out and to find something to eat. Aeneas' closest friend, Achates, lights a fire, and everyone clusters around trying to dry out the waterlogged grain and corn. Aeneas, however, is worried about the thirteen lost ships, for only seven managed to reach the shore with him. Leaving the others by the fire he climbs a bluff to see what he can see. There is no sign of a ship anywhere, but a herd of deer feeding on the shore catches his eye. He proceeds to shoot seven of them, one for each ship. While they all eat their first decent meal in days Aeneas attempts to fill them with hope and renewed courage by making a brief speech, although he does not quite possess this hope and courage himself. He is terribly worried, not knowing where they are, or what has happened to all the others.

COMMENT: This passage reveals another important aspect of Aeneas' character, his greatness of soul. His comrades only vaguely understand his mission, so that he must comfort them and urge them on toward the great goal even though he is utterly miserable himself. Perhaps this points up the greatest contrast between the Homeric heroes and those of Virgil. Homer's heroes do what their human nature compels them to do, but Virgil's act to fulfill their sense of duty. Thus this speech, taken with his cry in the storm, shows the basic forces of Aeneas' nature: 1) his respect for duty, 2) his firm resolution, and 3) his understanding of the sufferings of others.

NAMES AND PLACES

CERES: the goddess of harvest, crops, grain.

PHRYGIA: the ancient name for the country in Asia Minor where Troy was located. Here it is used instead of saying Troy.

TRINACRIAN SHORE: Sicily; the name came from the fact that Sicily has three promontories and is triangular in shape.

SCYLLA: a six-headed monster who lived on the Italian side of the strait of Messina (the narrow bit of water that separates Italy from Sicily). She would snatch six men at a time off any ship that sailed near enough.

CYCLOPS: Polyphemus, a one-eyed giant who lived on the eastern side of Sicily.

(LINES 223-417.) Meanwhile, back among the gods, it is Venus' turn to get upset. Aeneas is her son, and it seems to her that Jupiter has gone back on his promise to help the Trojans. Tearfully she approaches the king of the gods and reminds him that the Trojans are his chosen people since they are to found Rome. Venus reproaches him with the fact that another Trojan, Antenor, found a refuge in the north of Italy. Why should not Aeneas, who is his own grandson? Jupiter, smiling at her concern, comforts her with a prophecy of Rome's future greatness, and sends the messenger of the gods, Mercury, (the son of Maia) to the Carthaginians. He persuades them to be hospitable to the Trojans.

The next morning Aeneas sets out to investigate his whereabouts and meets his mother (Venus) disguised as a huntress. He does not recognise her, though he is fairly sure she is not mortal, but he asks her where he is. Venus tells him that he has landed in Africa near Carthage and that the queen of the country is Dido. She then describes the whole story of Dido's flight from Tyre; how Dido's brother Pygmalion, murdered her husband, Sychaeus, so that Dido had to flee in secret. At the end of the story Venus asks Aeneas who he is (to keep up the deception), and when he mentions his lost ships she interrupts with the information that they are safe. Then she turns to go, and as a parting gesture, dissolves her disguise: the short huntress tunic falls down to her feet, perfume fills the air, and Aeneas recognises his mother. He tries to keep her from going, but she vanishes after carefully veiling him and Achates in an invisible cloud. Concealed in this cloud, the two friends set out for Carthage.

COMMENT: The interview with Jupiter is an opportunity for Virgil to use one of his favorite poetic devices, contrast. Jupiter's un-ruffled calm is in sharp contrast to Venus' tears as well as a contrast to the tumult of the storm. The reader also becomes aware of the tremendous difference between the emotions of Jupiter and Juno. Jupiter is serene where Juno is passionate. But most important of all, the king of the gods is a symbol of what Rome, under Augustus, meant to Virgil. His powerful composure and kindly justice represent Rome's gift of law and order to the civilized world. Jupiter's speech gives Virgil his poetic opportunity to praise Rome and the great Augustus.

In addition to giving us a picture of Jupiter, this passage is important because in it occurs one of the most difficult words to put into English. That word is the adjective pius, rendered by many translators as good, and by a few as pious (its nearest English equivalent). Neither of these words is adequate because they make the reader think of Aeneas as a namby-pamby character. But to a Roman, the word pius was highest praise. It implied an eager willingness to fulfill one's duty to the gods, to parents, to the state, and to descendents. These duties were performed with a firmness of resolution which was noble and ungrudging. Thus the adjective pius and its corresponding noun, pietas, play a vital role in understanding the Aeneid.

NAMES AND PLACES

ILLYRIA, LIBURNIA, the river TIMAVUS: all located far up the Adriatic
Sea.   Antenor, escaping from Troy, sailed up the Adriatic and settled
near Padua.

CAESAR: here means Augustus. His whole name was Gaius Julius Caesar
Octavius Augustus.   Augustus, as Jupiter reveals toward the end of
his speech, was made a god even before he died. In later times Roman
emperors were usually not deified until after death.

RUTILIANS: the people living in Latium (in Italy) when Aeneas finally
landed there.   Aeneas had to defeat their King, Turnus, before he could
settle.

IULUS: another name for Aeneas' son Ascanius. The play with the various forms of Iulus' name is to remind the reader of the Julian house
and its ancestry.   Thus Augustus, adopted by Julius Caesar, is related
to Aeneas, the founder of the Roman race. (The Roman alphabet had
no J, but I was used as both consonant and vowel. In Medieval times
the consonantal I began to be written as a J.)

The RACE of HECTOR: the Trojans, so named because Hector was their
most famous hero.

VESTA: goddess of the sacred hearth fire which must always be kept
burning.   Her priestess, Rhea Silvia, was the mother (by the god Mars)
of Romulus and Remus. (Her father was the king of Alba Longa, Numitor, descended from Ascanius.)

PHTHIA: the home of the great Greek hero, Achilles, in Thessaly.

MYCENE and ARGOS: the homes of Agamemnon, the leader of the Greek
expedition to Troy, and Diomedes, both located in southern Greece.
The whole region became a Roman province in 146 B.C.

QUIRINUS: another name for Romulus.

GATES of WAR: gates of the temple of Janus which were closed during
times of peace, but open during war.   Augustus closed them in 29 B.C.
for the first time in nearly two hundred years.   Janus was the early
Italian god of entrances whose name is derived from the Latin word
meaning door.   He had two faces, one looking forward and the other
back.

HARPALYCE: a female warrior from Thrace.

SIST R of PHOEBUS APOLLO: Diana, goddess of the moon. Her favorite
sports were hunting and dancing.

AGENOR: founder of Sidon, the sister city of Tyre.

BYRSA: the Greek word for bull's hide.   Venus is describing the cir-
cumstances of the founding of Carthage.   The colonists had been granted
as much land as bull's hide could cover, so they cut the hide into thin
strips and thus traced out a large piece of land.

MT. OLYMPUS: the home of the gods, located in Thessaly.

AMBROSIA: usually the food of the gods, but here it is a perfume.

PAPHOS: a town on the west coast of Cyprus where a famous temple
to Venus was located.

(LINES 418-755.) Aeneas and his friend, Achates, still hidden in the cloud
which Venus had thrown around them, make their way along a path till they
finally reach Carthage. Here they admire the bustling energy of the workmen
who are still engaged in building; they are compared in a great simile to
bees around a hive. Arriving at Juno's magnificent temple, the two friends
are filled with even greater admiration, as well as distress: for on the
walls of the temple are huge murals depicting all the tragic events of the

fall of Troy. Aeneas himself appears in one painting. While they are gazing, overcome with sorrowful memories, the queen of Carthage, Dido, comes to the temple. She is accompanied by a great throng of citizens and princes, and behind them are the rest of Aeneas' followers from the thirteen lost ships. As Venus had promised him, they are safe. But of course no one sees Aeneas and Achates enfolded in their cloud!

After Dido has taken her seat near the temple door, various citizens approach her and make requests. She dispenses justice with calm dignity. Then the leader of the group of men from the lost ships, Ilioneus, comes forward from his position. He complains of inhositable treatment on the part of the Carthaginians, and says that he and his men are not looters or warriors. He begs permission to repair the battered ships so that they can be on their way. Dido apologizes, promising to help them, and even offers to let them stay in Carthage. At that moment, Aeneas, unable to stand it any longer, bursts out of his enveloping cloud and reveals himself. With a heart overflowing with gratitude, he begs the gods to reward Dido, the first person to show any pity and love for the Trojans. Dido responds graciously by inviting them all to a banquet at the palace. Immediately Aeneas sends Achates back to the ships to get everyone who was left behind, and especially to fetch his son, Ascanius.

But Venus, who has been keeping an eye on what has been going on and is still worried that Juno may try some new trick, decides that, for the Trojans to be really safe, Dido must fall in love with Aeneas. To accomplish this romance, she commands her son, Cupid, to assume the disguise of Ascanius (who is still a small boy). In the meantime she puts the real Ascanius to sleep. So Achates returns to the city, not with Ascanius, but with Cupid. The false Ascanius embraces his "father" and then climbs on Dido's lap. Poor Dido hasn't a chance! All during the banquet, and while the various Carthaginian princes are singing their ballads, she cannot take her eyes off Aeneas. Finally she persuades him to tell the story of his adventures during the seven years from the fall of Troy till he landed in Carthage. And with this forecast of the contents of Book II, the first book of the Aeneid comes to a close.

COMMENT: The closing portion of Book I contains two important poetic devices. The first of these, the simile, we have already met twice before. The third simile concerns one of Virgil's favorite subjects, bees. His great study of their habits occurs in the fourth book of the Georgics. The second device is the telling of the background of the story by means of pictures or reminiscence. Thus the past can be explained without breaking the thread of the present, while the reader gains a greater understanding of Aeneas' sorrows. Virgil in the murals is also recalling Homer, not only by referring to the chief characters of the Iliad, but also by echoing Homer's description of Achilles' shield with his own description of the murals. Virgil never ceases to be conscious of writing within the epic framework established by Homer.

NAMES IN PLACES

SONS OF ATREUS: Agamemnon and Menelaus, the chiefs of the Greeks together with Achilles, in the Trojan war. But Achilles refused to fight at first because he was angry with Agamemnon for taking his captive princess from him.

RHESUS: a Thracian king who was supposed to help the Trojans. An oracle had prophesied that the Greeks could not take Troy if the horses of Rhesus were to eat the grass around Troy and drink from its chief stream, the Xanthus. Unfortunately, Rhesus was killed by the Greeks and his horses seized by Odysseus and Diomedes (the son of Tydeus).

TROILUS: youngest son of Priam, king of Troy. He was killed by Achilles. The scene concerning Hector refers to Priam's ransoming Hector's body after Achilles had dragged it three times around the walls.

MEMNON: led the Ethiopean allies of Troy.

AMAZONS: a warrior nation of women whose queen, Penthesilea, came to the aid of the Trojans. She too was slain by Achilles.

EUROTAS: a river near Sparta in southern Greece.

MT. CYNTHUS: located on the Greek island of Delos and one of Diana's favorite spots. From the name of the mountain comes the other most common name of Diana, Cynthia. Her followers were the mountain nymphs, the Oreads.

HESPERIA: means Italy. The word is Greek for "Western Land."

OENOTRIA: another name for Italy, "Land of Vines."

ORION: the constellation which in the middle of summer rose near sunrise, and was thought to cause storms.

ACESTES: king of Sicily. He was friendly to the Trojans because his mother came from Troy.

TYRIAN TOWN: Carthage, since it was founded by settlers from Tyre.

FIELDS OF SATURN: a third name for Italy because Saturn was supposed to have ruled Italy in the Golden Age.

ERYX: another son of Venus. The country of Eryx means Sicily because Eryx, when king of Sicily built a temple to Venus on a mountain in the western part of the island.

PAROS: a Greek island in the Aegean Sea which provided the most beautiful white marble in antiquity. The passage in which this word occurs is an echo of lines 156-162 from Book XXIII of the Odyssey. Virgil has Aeneas emerging from the cloud; Homer has Odysseus emerging from the bath when he has finally reached his home. Both are clad in dazzling beauty by a goddess. Virgil, of course, assumes that his readers know the works of Homer.

TEUCER: not the founder of Troy here, but one of the sons of Telamon and a nephew of Priam. (His mother was Priam's sister, Hesione). When Teucer returned from Troy without his half-brother, Ajax, Telamon banished him to Cyprus. On the way he stopped off at Sidon to arrange terms with Belus (Dido's father) who was ruler of Cyprus.

PELASGIAN: means Greek here, although the term actually refers to the race which inhabited Greece in pre-historic times before the Greeks arrived.

HELEN: the famous wife of Menelaus, king of Sparta, who ran off with Paris, prince of Troy. Sparta was located in the Argive plain, as was Mycenae (ruled by Agamemnon).

PERGAMUM: the citadel, or inner stronghold, of Troy.

TYPHOEUS: a giant placed beneath a volcano by Jupiter's thunderbolts.

CYTHERA: an island off the southeastern part of Greece where a famous temple to Venus was located. Although some legends said she rose from the sea near Paphos, others said it was near Cythera.

IDALIUM: a town in Cyprus sacred to Venus.

ACIDALIAN MOTHER: Venus; the name came from the fountain, Acidalius, in Boeotia (central Greece) sacred to Venus and her followers, the three Graces.

BACCHUS: the well-known god of wine, whose favorite home was Thrace.

BITIAS: a Carthaginian noble.

TOPAS: another noble who was supposed to have been taught by Atlas, the legendary first astronomer. The mountain in northwestern Africa was named after him. Iopas' ballad concerns the eclipses of the sun. The ancients referred to them as "the toils of the sun" because they thought the sun was enduring great struggles at such a time.

ARCTURUS, HYADES, BEARS: three constellations. The Hyades were associated with rainy weather.

AURORA'S SON: Memnon; Aurora, goddess of the Dawn, married Priam's brother, Tithonus.

SUMMARY: The first book of the <u>Aeneid</u> serves to introduce several of the most important characters in the poem and to reveal its basic themes.

1. We learn something of the personality of Aeneas. This personality is to grow and change with the development of the epic: his sorrowful memory of the events in Troy and his yearning for the past; his noble spirit looking forward to Rome, shown by his willingness to undergo all trials in order to fulfill the destiny set by the gods; and his human feeling for the sufferings of others.

2. We learn a little about Dido's generosity and her impulsive actions of the heart. The appearance of Cupid is a foreshadowing of the love story which is told in detail in the fourth book.

3. We are introduced to the various roles of the gods: a.) Jupiter, the unruffled dispenser of law and order; b.) Juno, the goddess with unruly emotions, jealousy, anger, passionate love for her chosen people, the Carthaginians; c.) Venus, the watchful mother and protectress of Aeneas; d.) Neptune, powerful like his brother Jupiter, but not quite as serene, also on the side of the Trojans.

4. Lastly, the poet reveals his themes.

    a. The greatness and mission of Rome, symbolized by Aeneas, and given special emphasis by the fact that Rome is the last word in the first five introductory lines to the poem.

    b. The contrast of violence with order, emotion with self-control, seen in the personalities of the gods and mortals, and even in nature itself.

    c. The continuous awareness of the greatness of Homer. achieves this awareness by subtle references to the <u>Iliad</u> or <u>Odyssey</u>, or by almost word for word translations. However, Virgil has a concept of the Homeric tradition which he develops with a more spiritual insight. For Homer's heroes are pretty much men of the moment who act as their natures make them, but Virgil' characters always carry with them a sense of past and future, and act from duty, the noblest of Roman virtues.

BOOK II

(LINES 1-249.) The events of Books II and III are a flashback from Book I, In them Aeneas relates the tragedy of the fall of Troy (II) and the fortunes of the exiles on land and sea after they flee from Troy (III). At the end of the first book we left Aeneas when the banquet was over with an audience of Carthaginian nobles, waiting spellbound to hear his tale about the fall of Troy.

After ten years of fighting and getting nowhere, the Greeks, pretending to be discouraged, had withdrawn to the island of Tenedos, off the coast of Troy. They had left behind them, however, a huge wooden horse. When the Trojans, thinking the Greeks had sailed away, rushed out of the city with joy to see the abandoned camp they found the horse and were at a loss as to what to do. Some were for drowning it in the sea, others wanted to drag it into the city. The strongest voice against the horse was raised by the priest Laocoön. Ending his speech with the famous words "I fear the Greeks, even when they bring gifts," he hurled his spear at the horse's side. A great echo came forth, like a moan, but the rest of the Trojans were not convinced. And just at this point of indecision, some shepherds rushed forward with a young Greek prisoner.

Little did the Trojans suspect what trickery the Greeks could think up. For this man, Sinon, had let himself be captured so that he might persuade the Trojans to not fear the horse. Weaving a tall tale, Sinon told Priam (king of Troy) how it was that he came to be hated by Ulysses (Odysseus is his Greek name): Ulysses with his clever words had managed to persuade the sooth-sayer, Calchas, that Sinon was the cause of the Greeks' misfortunes in battle. When Calchas had appealed to the oracle of Apollo to ask what should be done, the answer came that just as the Greeks appeased the winds with the blood of a virgin (see under comment) in order to get to Troy, so another life must be sacrificed in order to leave. Obviously Sinon was the man. This was the reason for his running to the protection of Priam. The old king was completely taken in by the dreadful story, and begged Sinon to explain the existence of the horse. Swearing up and down that he hated the Greeks and would always hate them, Sinon said that the horse was an offering to Minerva (her Greek name is Athena). Minerva had been offended when Diomedes and Ulysses had touched her small wooden image (Palladium) with bloody hands and therefore caused the Greek fortunes to fall. To atone for this crime and to regain the goddess' favor, Calchas had told them to make a gigantic horse out of wood so big that the Trojans would not be able to get it inside their city wall. The poor Trojans believed every word.

To their horror, they then saw two huge serpents coming through the waves and heading straight for them as they were gathered around Laocoön, who was preparing to sacrifice a bull to Neptune. In a panic everybody fled, except Laocoön and his two sons. The serpents coiled around the two sons and choked them to death. Moments later Laocoön shared their fate, and their screams filled the air. To all the Trojans this seemed a sign that Minerva was angry with Laocoön for denouncing the horse, and so with much celebration and singing they dragged it into the city. Even then, there was one last chance to save themselves. Cassandra, Priam's daughter, rushed out to prophesy the dreadful things to come. But when Apollo had given her the ability to prophesy he cursed her at the same time because she had rejected him as a lover. The curse was that no Trojan would ever believe her. Little realizing the terrible events that would come with nightfall, the happy Trojans wreathed the temples of the gods throughout the city with garlands.

> **COMMENT:** Book II commences at a swift pace which gathers momentum as the battle scenes are portrayed and follow one another in swift imagery. It is a book of scenes, but it is a book containing individual portraits as well. In this first passage we have no trouble in imagining to ourselves either the traitor Sinon, or the tortured Laocoön. (In fact the vivid account in Virgil of the death-agony of father and sons was the subject of one of the most famous sculptures of the second half of the first century by three Rhodian sculptors, Agesander, Athenodorus, and Polydorus).

NAMES AND PLACES

MYRMIDONS and DOLOPIANS: soldiers of Achilles from Thessaly.

ULYSSES: known in Homer as "wily Odysseus" or "Odysseus of many schemes" went through many years of wandering around various parts of the Mediterranean after the Trojan war. Aeneas is therefore drawing a subtle comparison with his own adventures. Ulysses is also credited by legend with being the author of the plan for the wooden horse. His home was the island of Ithaca.

DANAANS: another poetic name for the Greeks, coming from the name of one of the early kings of Argos, Danaus.

ACHAEANS: another tribe of Greeks, dominant in the southern part. The word is often used by Virgil to mean all the Greeks.

DARDANIAN: equals Trojan, from Dardanus, a mythical ancestor of the Trojans.

PALAMEDES: earned Ulysses' hatred by proving that Ulysses was not mad. Ulysses, not wishing to join the expedition for Troy had pretended insanity. As evidence, he yoked a horse and a bull together to plough the seashore. Then he sowed it with salt. Clever Palamedes placed Ulysses' son, Telemachus, in the furrow, and Ulysses, seeing him, turned aside. To get his revenge, Ulysses later forged a letter from Priam to Palamedes which arranged for the latter to betray the Greeks. As further proof Ulysses hid some gold in Palamedes tent. Palamedes was therefore found guilty and put to death.

BELUS: son of Neptune, father of Aegyptus and Danaus, who, according to some traditions was king over Libya and Egypt.

THE VIRGIN: Iphigenia, daughter of Agamemnon, was sacrificed to Diana at Aulis (on the strait of Euboea) in order that the Greeks might have fair winds to Troy.

SON OF TYDEUS: Diomedes.

OMENS: Here Virgil is imposing the Roman custom of consulting the auspices on a Greek priest. It consisted of examining the entrails of animals, or of observing the way chickens pecked at corn which was thrown to them. The Romans rarely did anything without consulting auspices or omens. A tremendous amount of ritual was involved, and one little wrong step meant that the whole thing had to be done again.

TRITONIA: Minerva.

(LINES 250-558.) Night descended and inside the city everyone slept, believing that the Greeks had truly departed. They could not have been more wrong. The Greek fleet sailed stealthily in the moonlight back from Tenedos, where it had been hiding, to the Trojan shore. When the commander's ship had given the signal light, Sinon, who had been watching from within the walls, opened up the wooden horse and they proceeded directly to kill the men on watch and throw wide the gates to the rest of the Greeks. Meanwhile (Aeneas now brings himself into the story) the dead Trojan hero, Hector, appeared to Aeneas in a dream and warned him to escape. He must not even think of trying to organize a defense, as Troy was in flames. His parting words were to take his household gods, the Lares and Penates, with him as symbols of Troy to the new city which he was to establish.

But while Aeneas dreamt, Troy burned, and rousing himself hastily from sleep (as the hero tells us), he rushed out on the roof. The description of the fire is the chance for Virgil's first simile in Book II: picture a beautiful cornfield in flames while the wind rages; or imagine a flooded river pouring destruction on fields and flocks while from a safer, higher spot, the shepherd looks on helpless. Aeneas too, was helpless. As he stood there, a friend, Panthus, came up with the news that the Greeks were masters of Troy. This information so inflamed Aeneas that he dashed out into the fighting on the city streets, gathering a small group of loyal hearts as he went. Virgil compares these last brave Trojans to a pack of wolves, wild with long hunger. Thus they fought their way to the center of the city. There they met a band of Greeks who mistook them at first for friends. Too late they realized the error. The Greek leader, Androgeos, jumped back as if he had suddenly stepped on a snake. Aeneas and his group slaughtered the Greek band and took their armor.

So the battle surged till they came to the thickest part of the fighting around Priam's palace. No matter how many Greeks were killed by the missiles falling and being thrown, they still kept coming. Finally a Greek leader, Pyrrhus whom Virgil compares to a viper fed on poisonous herbs, sleek and slippery, forced the inner door and the horde swarmed into Priam's palace. Here Virgil again uses the comparison of a river swollen into a flood and overwhelming its banks to give vividness to the picture of the rush of the Greeks. Priam's wife Hecuba, together with her daughters, was slain beside the household altar. As the aged king himself was struggling to reach her and the sanctuary of the altar, one of his sons, Polites, fled by, trying to escape the word of Pyrrhus. Right in front of Priam, Pyrrhus caught up with his victim and stabbed him to death. Filled with anger and despair the weak king in vain hurled his spear, which of course bounced harmlessly off Pyrrhus' shield. Then slipping and sliding in the son's gore, Pyrrhus grabbed the old father by the hair of his head, and buried his sword up to the hilt in the king's body. Then he struck off the head and left the body there, a "corpse without a name."

COMMENT: This passage presents powerfully striking images and a sense of immediacy to the reader. In achieving this result, the similes play a very important role. There are six similes in little more than two hundred and fifty lines. Another way Virgil creates immediacy is by making his individual descriptions brief and by jumping quickly to the next. It is an effect similar to that of the modern movie camera in "swish-pan" shooting where the camera focuses on one spot and then swishes along the horizon line to the next, leaving the intervening objects in a rushed blurr to show that the two focused scenes are connected. This passage is also important in giving us the only picture of Aeneas before the awesome burden of his destiny fills his life. Here he is like one of Homer's heroes, eager for battle in spite of impossible odds.

NAMES AND PLACES

THE SPOILS OF ACHILLES: Hector killed Patroclus who was wearing Achilles' armor. The armor of a dead man belonged to his slayer.

PENATES: Aeneas took with him his own household gods, but these represented those of Troy. Hector also entrusted him with an image of Vesta, the goddess of the never-dying hearth fire.

DEIPHOBUS: the third of Priam's sons (Hector and Paris were the oldest). He married Helen after Paris was slain in battle, and therefore his house was the first to burn.

PERGAMUM: the inner stronghold of Troy.

ORCUS: the god of Death and also the Underworld, sometimes referred to as Pluto.

ANDROMACHE: wife of Hector. Their first-born son was named Astyanax, which in Greek means "lord of the city." One of the most touching scenes to modern readers in the Iliad is the description of Hector's farewell to his wife and son at the gates of the city. (Book VI, 370 ff.)

PYRRHUS: his other name is Neoptolemus. He was the son of Achilles, sent for after his father was killed by Paris, with Apollo's help.

SCYROS: an island in the Aegean which was the kingdom of Pyrrhus' grandfather, Lycomedes.

(LINES 558-804.) It was the horrible sight of Priam's death which brought Aeneas up short. He had been filled only with the rage to kill and to get even. But the violent death of the beloved king brought the image of Aeneas' own aged father to his mind. For the first time, also, he thought of his wife, Creusa, and their son Iulus. Looking around, he found himself deserted, and then suddenly spied the cause of all the trouble, Helen, daughter of Tyndareus. In terror of the Trojan's anger, she was hiding behind the altar. With a frenzied mind, Aeneas started for her, with intent to kill. But his ever watchful mother, Venus, appeared in a vision, radiantly beautiful, and prevented him with words about his father and his family. She told him that it was the ill-favor of the gods, not Helen or even Paris who had caused the destruction of Troy. The very gods themselves were taking sides with the Greeks: Neptune, Juno, Minerva, Jupiter. Aeneas looked around. The fall of Troy was like (and here follows one of Virgil's most famous similes) a huge tree on the top of the mountain which woodsmen have hacked away at for hours which finally crashes down with its roots all torn up.

But amid all the flames and fighting, Aeneas, under divine protection, made his way safely back to his own home. At first his father refused to be rescued, claiming that he was too old and had lived long enough. The whole house burst into tears trying to persuade him, but to no avail. Finally Aeneas started to rush off into the fighting again, and Creusa, holding up the small son in her arms, begged him at least to let them die with him. But as she spoke a miraculous omen occured. A tiny flame appeared over Iulus' head and set his hair on fire. But the holy flames did not hurt him, although the anxious mother put them out as quickly as she could. To the old father, Anchises, however, it was a sign. He resisted the entreaties of his son no longer. Two other omens followed: a thunderbolt and a shooting star. Without wasting any more time, Aeneas took his father on his shoulders and his son by the hand, while Creusa followed behind. Their destination was a small hill outside the city where an ancient temple of Ceres stood. To prevent Aeneas' pollution of the sacred household images (since he had just come from battle) Anchises was to carry them. But the story was not to have such a happy ending. For Aeneas, hearing the sound of pursuing Greeks close at hand, took a few back alleys and shortcuts, and arrived at Ceres' temple; only Creusa was not with them.

Leaving his father and son there, Aeneas, totally distraught, retraced his steps back to the burning city, calling loudly for Creusa. There was no answer. Suddenly, Creusa's ghost appeared and told him it was not the will of the gods that she should go with him. He would find a royal wife in Hesperia (Italy) and a fortunate turn of events; even a kingdom. Her last words were to take care of their child. Aeneas tried to put his arms around her but she vanished, and there was nothing else for him to do but to go back to his father and son and the other Trojans who had gathered with them. Thus Aeneas shouldered his burden of leadership, and the exiles departed.

> **COMMENT:** In this passage we see one of Virgil's most important poetic affects, the swift change of mood. Up to the death of Priam we have been conscious only of the glory of war. Even the burning city is something splendid. But after the brutal slaying of the king of Troy, we become conscious only of the horror of war. It is this sense of horror that forces Aeneas to surrender himself to his destiny, which was first foretold him by Hector in the dream and later repeated by the ghost of Creusa. Aeneas has thus changed from a Homeric hero living almost entirely in the present, to a Virgilian hero constantly aware of both past and future.

NAMES AND PLACES

TYNDAREUS: husband of Leda but not actually Helen's father. Leda was her mother, Jupiter her father.

FURIES: the avenging deities of crimes toward parents, murder, and the like. They were said to take away all peace of mind and to lead their victims to wretched misfortune. (The Greek word for them is Erinyes).

NEPTUNE: not only the sea god, but the builder of Troy for Laomedon. Now he is going to help destroy his creation.

SCAEAN GATE: the most important gate into Troy.

PHOENIX: Achilles' aged tutor.

LYDIAN TIBER: Tradition holds that the area around the Tiber and just north of it, where the Etruscans lived, was colonized by the Lydians from Asia Minor.

MOTHER OF THE GODS: Cybele, the Great Mother goddess of Asia Minor. She is also known as Rhea.

SUMMARY: Book II has two important functions.   1.) In it Virgil reveals his ability to create scenes that are immediately visible to the imagination of the reader.   We are consistantly aware of the turmoil of battle and the determination of the warriors.   2.)   The second function of the book is to make the reader realize what a horrible memory it is that Aeneas has to carry with him on his long journey to found a new city. The fierce heat of the flames, the screams, the lost wife, the king slaughtered in the still warm blood of his son, all these were ever present in Aeneas' mind. No wonder the process of forgetting took so long. The ability to lay these aside, and the courage and dedication to go on to build a city with a mighty future, make Aeneas a great hero.

BOOK III

(LINES 1-293.) Book III continues the flashback begun in Book II. Aeneas is still relating the story of what happened after the collapse of Troy. By early summer Aeneas and the few men who had managed to escape the burning city had constructed a fleet. In ancient times no one ever sailed directly across an open body of water if it were possible to sail close to the coast. So the first place they landed at was Thrace, which has long been friendly to Troy. There Aeneas founded a city Aeneadae. But as he was about to sacrifice to Venus and was starting to pull up some sapplings of myrtle to garland the altar, blood seemed to drip from the bark. Then came a moan and a voice asking why was he disturbing the grave of Polydorus, who had been sent by his father Priam to the king of Thrace. When Agamemnon conquered and the power of Troy was no longer great, the Thracian king had slain him. Because of such a dreadful omen, it was quite obvious to Aeneas that they could not stay where they were any longer. After performing new funeral rites to quiet the unhappy ghost, the Trojan exiles took to their ships again.

The next shore they reached was the island of Delos, birthplace of Apollo and Diana. There the king, Anius, welcomed them and Aeneas sought the advice of Apollo's oracle. As was usual, the oracle's answer was not very clear: he was to seek out the land from which their race had originally sprung. Anchises assumed that this meant Crete because there was a Mt. Ida on Crete as well as near Troy. Legend also said that Teucer, the founder of the Trojan race, came from Crete to Troy. Joyfully the Trojans left Delos and with a following breeze they soon sighted the coast of Crete.

A second time they set to work to build a city. This time they named it Pergamum after the inner citadel of Troy. But misfortune was not far off. A dreadful disease attacked both men and crops, accompanied by scorching drought. Anchises advised them to return to Delos and obtain another oracle. But one night in a dream the sacred household gods which Aeneas had brought from Troy appeared to him and told him that the promised land was Hesperia, otherwise known as Italy. It filled the qualifications of being the land from which the founder of the Trojan race came because Iasius, who was born in Italy, had married one of Teucer's daughters. When Aeneas revealed this dream to his father, Anchises recalled that Cassandra had prophesied that Italy was their goal. But of course, due to Apollo's curse, no one had ever believed her.

Again they set sail and after a storm which lasted three days and nights they sight land: the two islands of the Strophades in the Ionian Sea, west of Greece. Bad luck was to be followed by worse, for these islands were inhabited by winged creatures with women's faces, known as Harpies. Whatever they touched became unclean. Thus when Aeneas and his followers killed some of the goats and cattle they found feeding on the grass (they probably had little if anything to eat during the three day storm and were ravenous) the Harpies swooped down and contaminated everything, including the sacrifice on the altar. Hastily Aeneas told everyone to try and fight the winged things off. The hideous creatures flew away, but their leader, Celaeno, paused on a high cliff to curse them. She cried that they would reach Italy, but that they would not build the walls of their city till hunger forced them to devour the very tables on which they ate. Everyone wanted to leave such a horrible place as quickly as possible, so they hastily got underway.

After sailing up the western coast of Greece past the island home of Ulysses, Ithaca, they made a brief stop at Actium. There they held a festival of games and wrestling, and then pushed on further north till they came to Chaonia, where they found friends.

> **COMMENT:** In this passage the reader cannot help but have a slight feeling of unreality about the serious nature of Aeneas' adventures. Perhaps this is because Virgil, in trying to follow Homeric footsteps, did not really believe these adventures would increase the greatness of his hero. Whatever the reason, the events somehow lack the vividness of the scenes in Book II.

NAMES AND PLACES

LYCURGUS: persecuted Bacchus and his kingdom therefore became sterile; its fertility returned after his exposure on a mountain.

DIONE: daughter of Earth and Sky, loved by Jupiter, and thus mother of Venus.

NYMPHS: the Hamadryades, or nymphs of the groves who lived in trees. They symbolized the spirit of the tree for they were born with it, and died when it died. As lesser goddesses, Aeneas first worships them, and then Gradivus (Mars) the more important divinity of Thrace. (Getic means Thracian, since the Getae were one of the Thracian tribes.)

NEREIDS: There were fifty of them, nymphs of the Mediterranean, daughters of Doris and Nereus.

GYAROS AND MYCONOS: two islands in the group known as the Cyclades. Legend runs that Apollo was supposed to have moored Delos, because it was so tiny to the two larger islands of Gyaros and Myconos.

PHOEBUS: another name for Apollo.

THYMBRA: a place near Troy where Apollo had a famous temple.

RHOETEAN: here means Trojan after the name of a small promontory north of Troy called Rhoeteum.

CYBELE: a mountain, sacred to the goddess of the same name, located in Phrygia.

CORYBANTES: followers of Cybele who performed her rites with clashing cymbals and wild dancing. Lions were harnessed to her chariot.

GNOSSOS: (Knossos in Greek spelling) the most important city in Crete.

ZEPHYRUS: the west wind.

IDOMENEUS: Cretan leader who took part in the Trojan war. On his way home a storm came up and he foolishly vowed to Neptune the first living creature that he should meet if he arrived safely. Naturally the first thing he met was his son. Obediently he sacrificed him, but a plague followed. So Idomeneus fled from Crete to settle in Italy.

ORTYGIA: an earlier name for Delos.

NAXOS: the island where Theseus deserted Ariadne after slaying the Minotaur in Crete. She was rescued by Bacchus, and therefore the island was sacred to him.

DONYSA, OLEAROS, PAROS: all islands of the group known as Cyclades.

CURETES: the name for the priests of Jupiter in Crete, where he was worshipped with noisy rites. He had been hidden on the island when a baby to escape being killed by his father, Cronos. His cries were covered up by the Curetes clashing their arms.

PERGAMUM: Virgil connects the historical town of Pergamum with
    Aeneas.
DARDANUS and IASIUS were brothers: Both married daughters of Teucer
    who was king in Asia Minor.
CORYTHUS: an ancient town in Etruria, north of the Tiber river.
AUSONIA: another name for Italy.
DICTAEAN: means Cretan from the name of the mountain, Dicte, in Crete.
PALINURUS: the pilot.
PHINEUS: a king of Thrace whom the gods punished by sending the Harpies
    to destroy his house.   But two of the famous Argonauts (sailors of the
    ship Argo who went in search of the golden fleece), Zetes and Calais,
    drove the Harpies off.
STYGIAN WAVES: referring to the river Styx of the Underworld, where
    monsters lived.
LAOMEDON: organized the building of Troy, but refused to pay Apollo
    and Neptune for their work.   The Harpy, Calaeno, is taunting the Trojans
    by reminding them that they are descended from a man famous for breaking
    his word.
ZACYNTHUS, DULICHIUM: islands off the western coast of Greece.
NERITUS: mountain of Ithaca.
SAME: town on the island of Cephallenia.
MT. LEUCATA: a mountain sacred to Apollo on the southern tip of the
    island of Leucadia.
BUTHROTUM: located in the region of Chaonia in northern Epirus.

(LINES 294-718.) Having arrived at the city of Buthrotum, Aeneas heard
the rumor that one of Priam's sons, Helenus, was the ruler. He had been
captured in the Trojan war by Pyrrhus and after the latter's death received
a portion of the kingdom and Andromache (first married to Hector, and then
to her captor, Pyrrhus) as wife. Sure enough, the first person Aeneas met
was Andromache weeping by the river Simois (named after the Trojan River).
She told him all that had happened to her since her capture by Pyrrhus.
At this point, Helenus himself came out of the city, thrilled to find some
fellow Trojans. Aeneas, after a few days rest, decided to go to Helenus
(he possessed prophetic powers) and find out if he knew the will of Apollo
and if he could advise him how to avoid more misfortunes. Helenus gave
a lengthy answer. He told Aeneas that though Italy seemed very close, a
long journey was still ahead of him, for the western coast of Italy was his
destination. To get there he would have to face the two perils of Scylla
and Charybdis. These monsters guarded the Strait of Messina between
Italy and Sicily. Scylla had six heads with which she snatched men from
unsuspecting ships which came too close to the Italian shore. Charybdis was
a whirlpool on the Sicilian side which sucked the ships down as they tried
to escape from Scylla. Therefore, though it was much shorter to go through
the strait, Helenus advised Aeneas to go the long way around the southern
coast of Sicily. Above all, he must remember to reverence Juno and perform
all the proper ritual to keep her favor. When they reached Cumae (near
Naples) they were to seek counsel from the Sibyl there. She would tell them
what the future would bring. When Helenus had given his advice he heaped
gifts on the travelers, while Andromache gave a scarf of her own to Aeneas'
son.

Everything went well as they crossed the small body of water between
Epirus and Italy, and on sighting this longed-for country, Anchises filled
a huge bowl with wine. Raising it on high to the gods, he prayed for their

continued favor. They made a short stop to sacrifice to Juno, as they had been warned, but the sight of white horses on the hillside appeared as an omen of war. So they set sail again. They came to the fateful whirlpool of Charybdis and just barely managed to avoid it.

But a new danger faced them, for they beached their ships on the coast of Sicily which was the home of the Cyclops, huge one-eyed giants. Over the whole region towered the mighty volcano, Aetna. After hiding in the woods all night, they were startled by the grotesque figure of a young man, all in tatters and wild-looking, who rushed toward them. Grovelling piteously he begged them to take him along. He, Achaemenides, was one of Ulysses' companions, who had been left behind when Ulysses made his escape from the Cyclops, Polyphemus. For three months he had been living off berries and roots. Even if they were to kill him, it would still be better than being eaten by a Cyclops. As he spoke, Polyphemus appeared in the distance. Even though he could not see the Trojans on the shore (Ulysses had put out his one eye) he heard the noise of the oars in the water. He headed for the sound and waded far out into the sea. The fleet had gotten just out of reach. Polyphemus let out a roar of anger which summoned all the other Cyclops to the shore. They towered raging at the waters edge while the Trojans threw on all sail.

This was their last adventure till they got to Drepanum on the western tip of Sicily because Achaemenides was able to give them helpful information about the Sicilian coast. But Aeneas was not to leave Drepanum without suffering another sorrow—the loss of his father—for which he was completely unprepared. It was after leaving Drepanum that the storm arose (the point at which Virgil begins the tale in Book I) which drove them to the shores of Carthage. Aeneas finishes his story at last; the banquet is over.

COMMENT: In spite of the number of events in this passage, the reader still does not get the impression that Aeneas has really been through very much. The most important fact is the warning about Juno, which reminds us that it was Juno's anger in Book I which caused the storm to drive Aeneas off his course. But Juno could not for a long time bring herself to be friendly to Aeneas, and not yet could he found Rome.

NAMES AND PLACES

HERMIONE: the only child of Menelaus, king of Sparta (Lacedaemon), and Helen (daughter of Leda and Jupiter). She had been promised to Orestes, son of Agamemnon and Clytemnestra. But when Clytemnestra had murdered her husband when he returned from Troy, Orestes had taken revenge by killing the murderess. For this crime of matricide the Furies drove Orestes mad. (See Aeschylus, Oresteia.)

CLARIAN: adjective from Claros referring to Apollo, because at Claros in Asia Minor there was a temple and an oracle dedicated to Apollo. The laurel was a bush sacred to the god and his priestess sat on the tripod when the oracle was consulted.

CIRCE: a sorceress who changed her guests into beasts, but from whom Ulysses managed to escape, fled from her island Aea, to a promontory off the coast of Latium.

LAKES: the marshy area round Avernus in Southern Italy was thought to be an entrance into the Lower World.

LOCRIANS: colonizers of Southern Italy from Narycium on the mainland of Greece opposite Euboea. According to legend they were driven by storms to south Italy after the Trojan war. The historical fact is that all of southern Italy along the coast was settled in the ninth, eighth, and seventh centuries by Greeks. The area was known as Magna Graecia.

LYCTOS: a city in Crete.

SALLENTINI: a people inhabiting the southernmost tip of Italy.

PHILOCTETES: a Greek hero from Meliboea in Thessaly who took part in the Trojan war. His claim to fame was killing Paris.

PETELIA: another city in southern Italy, said to have been founded by Philoctetes.

PELORUS: northeastern promontory of Sicily on the strait of Messina.

PACHYNUS: southernmost point of Sicily.

SIBYL: a prophetess whose utterances were written on palm leaves. Aeneas is warned by Helenus not to let any breeze scatter the leaves, for then the prophecy would be unreadable.

DODONA: the location of most ancient of all the oracles of Greece, in Epirus.

MINERVA'S HEIGHT: a hill at the tip of the "heel" of Italy. The modern name is Castro.

LACINIUM: a headland on the east coast of Bruttium on which was a temple of Juno.

CAULON and SCYLACEUM were cities further along the coast of Italy.

ENCELADUS: one of the giants who fought against the gods.

SICANIAN BAY: the bay of Syracuse.

ALPHEUS: the god of the river of the same name in Greece which flows into the Ionian Sea near Olympia. He was pursuing the nymph, Arethusa, and Diana, to save her, changed her into a fountain on the island of Ortygia in the Syracusan harbor. The river-god still chased her under the sea to Ortygia, trying to mingle his stream with her waters.

CAMERINA: a Sicilian city which had been warned by an oracle never to drain the marsh near by. When the inhabitants disobeyed, the enemy entering by the drained marsh was able to capture the town. All the proper names in this final section of the book are cities in Sicily. Near two of them, Drepanum and Lilybaeum, famous battles in the First Punic War took place. (Rome against Carthage 260-256 B. C.)

SUMMARY: The tale of Aeneas' travels, after the excitement of the fall of Troy is something of a disappointment to the reader. The book is full of names, places and events, similar to those in Homer's Odyssey, but it lacks the vigorous flavor of adventure. This is partly due to the fact that oracles always announce what is going to happen ahead of time, so that there is little sense of suspense. It is also due to the fact that the gods are removed from any direct action. True, Aeneas consults Apollo's oracle, and sacrifices to Jupiter and Juno, but these gods do not themselves have anything to do with what happens. The apparent function of telling how Aeneas got from Troy to Carthage is the least important reason for the book. Virgil is really more concerned with unhappy recollections of the past (in the persons of Polydorus or Andromache, for instance) and the revelations concerning the future, which take place one after the other, rather than with the adventures themselves. But disappointing as the book is in many ways, it is still necessary in that it shows how much of a Trojan Aeneas still is, and how much a part of the Homeric tradition the Aeneid is.

BOOK IV

(LINES 1-197.) We are now back to where we were in Book I, and queen Dido is suffering as only these wounded by love can suffer. After tossing and turning all night, going over and over in her mind Aeneas' words and remembering his every look and gesture, she runs to her sister, Anna, for counsel. To Anna Dido confesses that if she had not made up her mind to remain loyal to her long dead husband, Sychaeus, she would be more than willing to yield to this intense emotion she now feels. She had truly loved Sychaeus and now she recognizes an awakening of those long dead feelings. No, she will never break her former vows. But as she utters these noble words she bursts into tears on Anna's shoulder. Anna, wanting her sister's happiness and also the welfare of Carthage, says that she thinks Dido has remained a widow long enough. Reminding Dido of the numerous enemies around Carthage, she subtly suggests that marriage with Aeneas would bring glory to the city.

They decide to sacrifice to all the gods who might make such a happy event take place. Ceres, Apollo, and Bacchus are each given a sheep because they are connected with marriage rites. But to Juno, the guardian of women, whose special concerns were wedlock and childbirth, Dido sacrifices a pure white heifer. Radiantly beautiful, the queen performs all the necessary ritual of examining the entrails of the victims, as each day she goes through the same ceremonies. But ceremonies to the gods have no meaning for a woman whose whole being is focused on the love of a man. "Dido burns," are the words of Virgil. She wanders around the city in a fog of unreality. She is like a deer which wanders through the woods, crazed by the pain of an arrow firmly stuck in her side.

As an excuse to be with Aeneas she takes him on sightseeing tours of the city. Every time she begins to say something, however, the words choke in her throat. Every night they dine together and, unable to make conversation, she makes him repeat the same story of his adventures over and over again. Then, when everyone is gone, she is again left alone with the unending thoughts and wishes going round and round in her head. In her mind's eye she sees him beside her; oh, so clearly. She even tries the ruse of making his son, Ascanius, fond of her so that Aeneas may take notice. The queen, in her anguish, forgets the city entirely. All the buildings to be constructed, the military training of the young men, every scheme for the beautifying and strengthening of Carthage is abandoned.

It isn't long before Juno becomes aware of the consuming passion of her beloved Dido. She goes to Venus, since it was the latter who started the whole affair (see the end of Book I) and proposes marriage as the only fair solution. Carthage and its inhabitants would be Dido's dowry. But Venus isn't so easily fooled. Knowing that Juno wants to keep Aeneas from reaching Italy, she says she really does not know what is best to do, and maybe Jupiter should be consulted. Juno then unfolds her plan that the two should go hunting. In the middle of the hunt she will cause a storm and, when Dido and Aeneas come to a cave for shelter, she, Juno, will join them in wedlock. Venus finally consents.

At the crack of dawn the next day the gay hunting party sets out. What a procession! Prancing horses, hunting dogs, spears with points sparkling in the sunlight, and lastly the lovely queen, splendid in purple, carrying a gold quiver, all process out of the gates. But as beautiful as Dido is, just as beautiful is Aeneas. The only being he can be compared to is the god, Apollo, when he sets out from his winter home to visit the island of Delos. Even young Ascanius has a horse and gallops about, hoping to get a boar at least. But the hunt is not long in progress when the storm, contrived by Juno, breaks. The rain and hail scatters the group all over the place, and "Dido and the Trojan leader arrive at the same cave." The only attendants at this wedding are the forces of nature. For marriage torches there is only lightning. For the wedding hymn there is the wailing of wood-nymphs (for thus Dido thinks of the moaning of the storm-tossed trees). In her mind she sees Juno and mother Earth as divine witnesses of the long desired event. To Dido it is a wedding, but to the outside world it is a sin. The evil goddess, Rumor, takes care of that. Nothing in the world travels as fast as Rumor with her countless eyes, ears and never silent mouths. Her power is so great that she can strike terror into mighty cities. Sometimes her words are true, but just as often, they are false. Now gleefully she spreads the gossip: Dido and Aeneas are lovers!

COMMENT: In this passage events move quickly, and all too realistically to their unavoidable conclusion. The feeling of tragedy, which increases as the story progresses, is present even in the opening lines of the book. With what skill Virgil accomplishes this! He portrays Dido not as a wicked woman of passion, but as a radiantly beautiful queen who falls in love because of her longing for heroic greatness. The nobility of Aeneas touches a responsive chord in her soul. Yet how clearly we see the power of love in the simile of the wounded deer. The very words Virgil uses show that the two were destined for this tragic love. For when he describes Aeneas, he compares him to Apollo in the same manner that he had compared Dido to Apollo's twin sister, Diana, in Book I. The adjective, pulcherrimus, (meaning extraordinarily beautiful) is used in the masculine form for Aeneas, and in its feminine form for Dido. We tend to shy away from using the word, beautiful, for a man. To the Greeks and Romans, however, it had no bad association. In telling what happened in the cave, Virgil shows tremendous insight and understanding. It affected Aeneas very little; so he is barely mentioned. It was not a formal wedding, but Dido's believing that it was and her wanting it to be so gave it a reality for her. At such times a woman always believes that the presence of the divine has sanctified her actions. The last dramatic image in the passage is that of exulting Rumor. This too, is so true of life. Almost before the deed occurs, everyone knows about it. Slowly the tragedy deepens.

NAMES AND PLACES

EREBUS: a lesser divinity, whose name signifies darkness and is therefore applied to the gloomy area through which the shades must pass on their way to the underworld.

IARBAS: the king of Gaetulia which boarded on Dido's Carthage. He had sought her hand in marriage but was refused.

SYRTES: two gulfs on the eastern half of the north African coast. They
were unfriendly due to their quicksands and exposure to the north winds,
the rocky shore, and variable tides.
BARCAEANS: wild tribes of the desert of North Africa.
LYAEUS: another name for Bacchus.
MASSYLIANS: a North African tribe from the area west of Carthage.
LYCIA: district on the southwest of Asia Minor.
DRYOPES: a people living in Asia Minor.
AGATHYRSI: tribe from Sarmatia on the Danube.   The various names
of these tribes are used to show that peoples from the ends of the earth
worshipped Apollo.
JUNO AND MOTHER EARTH: represent gods of sky and earth. Here
they perform the function of taking the auspices, a ceremony which
proceeded a wedding.   Juno also acts as the pronuba, the matron who
conducted the bride to the bridal room.
COEUS AND ENCELADUS: giants, known as Titans, who scaled Mt.
Olympus. They were sons of Mother Earth. When one brood of Titans,
represented by Coeus, was hurled down from the mountain, Earth, in anger,
produced another crop, of whom Enceladus was one.

(LINES 198-449.) When the story reaches Iarbas, Dido's rejected suitor,
he becomes thoroughly upset. Raising his hands to his father, Jupiter Ammon,
he complains that he has been dreadfully misused. It was he who gave Dido
the parcel of ground on which to settle, and yet she could spurn him and then
open her arms to Aeneas.   What sort of justice was this? Jupiter is moved
and sends Mercury to do something about the situation. After all, Aeneas
was not saved from burning Troy for the arms of a woman. So Mercury is
to remind Aeneas of his destiny and tell him to sail at once. And what
does he find the great hero doing, but building palaces and temples for
Carthage. The god reproaches him for being under Dido's thumb and forgetting his own glorious future. Even if the promise of his own kingdom in
Italy does not move him, at least he should remember his son's future.
Aeneas quickly comes to himself, but is now faced with the awful predicament:
how to tell Dido. One plan after the next occurs to him, but none of them are
any good. Finally he tells his men to ready the fleet, using utmost secrecy.
When Dido seems to be in the right mood, he will tell her.

But women in love are not so easily deceived. The preparations for sailing
do not escape her. Like a drunken Maenad in the orgies of Bacchus she
accosts Aeneas with the age-old words of reproach: how will she live,
what will she do, what of the enemies on all sides, her brother Pygmalion
who murdered her father, or the furious rejected king, Iarbas? What has
she done to be so treated?   As a last ruse she suggests the possibility that
she is carrying his child.

Aeneas is moved to terrible anguish with compassion for Dido and her grief
but he has no alternative. He did not seek her, but she went after him. His
love for the gods, for his father, for his son, must come first. Her complaining
only makes things worse for both of them. "Not of my own free will do I pursue
Italy."

Needless to say, these words are small comfort. A tirade of despair pours
forth from her lips: he is not the son of a goddess, but the son of hard gran-
ite.   She welcomed him when a beggar thrown on the shores by the storms.

Now she has become the beggar. He will rue the day, however, for she will haunt him wherever he goes. Even when she is dead, her ghost will never leave him. In utter agony she breaks off the flow of words and flees to her bed. Aeneas goes to look after the preparations for departure, sorrowful but determined. The men are eagerly at work, like ants. (A wonderful simile of the busy, tireless work of ants, follows). Slowly but surely all Dido's regal pride and self-respect leave her as she sees this energy which promises that Aeneas is going. Again and again she tries to get him to change his mind. Finally she goes to her sister to beg her to use her influence with him. If Anna could at least persuade him not to leave till the more favorable spring weather comes, she would be satisfied. But Anna's words can not move the heroic greatness of Aeneas, anymore than the strong north winds, with all their buffeting, can uproot a mighty oak tree. Still the hero has human qualities for, in spite of all, the scene, which could end with him appearing so cruel, ends with him weeping also.

COMMENT: This passage is important for the understanding of the character of both Dido and Aeneas. Dido, in breaking her vows to her dead husband, lost her self-respect. When her love, which was the reason for breaking the vows in the first place, is treated as worthless her only choice is death. Several times she hints at this death, the final time being in her speech to Anna. Her self-respect is the core of her nature and this is what makes her tragedy so great. As for Aeneas, we see both his humanity and his heroic greatness, if we read with understanding. He is no heartless cad, as we might think at first glance. For one brief moment he was happy, caught up in the affairs of the present and free of the burdens of past (Troy) and future (Rome). But men with a destiny seem not to be allowed happiness. The true importance of the oak tree simile is its emphasis on suffering, for Aeneas suffers in having to leave Dido. With reason does Virgil use the adjective pius to describe the hero as he determines to go. His sense of duty to gods and ancestors and descendants (all this is implied in the word pius) is what gives him the strength to carry out his resolution. His heart may be divided, but his duty is plain. In that is Aeneas' tragedy.

NAMES AND PLACES

AMMON: god of the Egyptian city of Thebes. The Romans later identified him with Jupiter. He was the father of Iarbas by a Libyan (Garamantean) nymph.

PARIS: Iarbas, in contempt, compares Aeneas to Paris because he is the successful suitor of another man's wife.

MAEONIAN: north-eastern portion of Lydia, bordering on Phrygia. Here Virgil thinks of it as Phrygian.

CYLLENIUS: a name for Mercury because he was born on Mt. Cyllene in Arcadia. His mother, Maia, was the daughter of Atlas. Virgil personifies the mountain, Atlas, which marked the western limit of the known world to the ancients.

ELISSA: another name for Dido.

HYRCANEA: a province in Persia along the south-eastern shore of the Caspian Sea.

ANCHISES: there was a legend that Diomedes stole the ashes of Anchises but later restored them to Aeneas.

THYIADS: Attic women (from near Athens) who worshipped Bacchus on Mt. Parnassus in Thebes in wild rites. The orgies were accompanied by waving a wand (the thyrsus) twined with ivy and topped by a pine cone, and clashing cymbals. Music was furnished by a flute-like instrument.

(LINES 450-705.) When there is no possible hope, Dido seeks death. As omens of this sad end she sees the holy water on the altars grow dark and the wine poured out to the god become blood. She tells no one of the dreadful sign. A second portent is the sound of her dead husband's voice coming from the marble chapel she had dedicated to him. Even the owl, screeching at night seems to foretell evil. Every night she dreams that Aeneas is haunting her, hounding her, the way the Furies hounded Orestes. Slowly the scheme for death evolves in her mind. Going to Anna, she tells her that she has decided to use the forces of magic to rid herself of this all-consuming love. A priestess from Ethiopia is to help her. She wants Anna to have a huge pyre built and to place on it the bed that she and Aeneas had shared, and the armor and clothes he had left behind. Anna suspects nothing and carries out her sister's wishes. Dido herself checks everything and arranges Aeneas' possessions carefully on the bed. The priestess calls upon the gods of the magical number three, Hecate and Diana, and the gods of the underworld, Erebus and Chaos. All the proper charms of love and sorcery are used: herbs cut in the moonlight with bronze sickles filled with black poison, and the forelock of a colt taken at birth. Dido herself stands at the altar wearing only one sandal and her clothes hanging down unbelted. Everything is set for the ceremony next day.

Night comes, but it brings sleep neither to Dido nor to Aeneas. Round and round go the thoughts in the head of the tortured queen of Carthage. Perhaps she should marry one of the Numidian princes, or maybe she could follow the Trojan ships to Italy; but they would never welcome her. If only she had never become involved with such a passion in the first place. As she was tossing, racked by indecision, Aeneas was snatching his last night's rest on the poop deck. Naturally he dreams: a god, looking like Mercury, appears, and warns him to set sail instantly. Dido is planning to burn their ships before they can get away. Without wasting a moment Aeneas rouses all his men, gives the order to cut the cables, and they are away, churning up the waters. When Dido looks out from the watch-tower at the first streak of dawn, she sees the sails white and full in the distance. Cursing herself for her inability to have ordered the Trojans slain, her indecision when she could have set fire to Aeneas' camp, she calls upon the gods to hear her evil prophecy. Aeneas will come to an untimely death and lie unburied in the sand, and never, never will there be any possibility of friendship between the nation that he should found and her kingdom.

These words hurled at heaven bring an end to her irresolution. She tells her old nurse, Barce, to go and get Anna and to make sure that she is ritually cleansed for the ceremony of burning the great pyre. The nurse leaves Dido and she, made strong at last with her dreadful purpose, climbs the funeral pyre. Collapsing on the bridal bed she reviews the past and begs to be released from her woes. She has built the city of Carthage and thus avenged her husband's murder. All would have been well, and she would have been happy, if the Trojan ships had never been blown to her shores. "I have lived," she says, "and accomplished the course of life which fortune gave." Before any of the watchers realizes what is happening, she stabs herself and falls back in a faint. Loud wails fill the air. Anna comes running. Too late it dawns on her why the pyre was built. Scrambling up she tries frantically to stem the flow of blood, and her robe grows red. Three times Dido tries to rise up on her elbow. Finally she moans in pain, and Juno, pitying her, sends her messenger Iris (the rainbow goddess) to release the soul from the tortured body. Gently the goddess cuts a few golden hairs from the queen's head to symbolize her sacrifice to the gods of the underworld. Dido breathes her last.

> **COMMENT:** This passage is filled with the presence of death, although Dido puts it off as long as she possibly can. The longer she delays, however, the more degraded she becomes. Her inner knowledge of this degradation increases the tragedy. But when she finally steels herself to the inevitable deed, once more she becomes a majestic queen and returns to the greatness she had when we first met her in Book I, dispensing justice before the temple of Juno. Through death, the poet defeats passion, while Aeneas, with still another sorrow added to his burden, sails on to fullfill his destiny.

NAMES AND PLACES

PENTHEUS: a king of Thebes who hid himself so that he could watch the mysteries of Bacchus. He was discovered, and torn to pieces. His madness caused him to see everything double.

EREBUS AND CHAOS: gods of the underworld especially associated with magic.

HECATE: she was associated with the moon, in the heavens, with Diana on earth, and with Persephone (the queen of the underworld) under the earth. Thus she was thought to have three heads, that of a horse, a dog, and a lion. She was worshipped at places where three roads met, and came to be regarded as the goddess of witchcraft. The passage which follows is full of magical lore which had a long literary tradition.

TITHONUS: brother of Priam who received the gift of immortality from the gods, due to the prayers of Aurora, goddess of the Dawn. But he was not given eternal youth, and eventually shriveled up with old age. In pity, Aurora changed him to a grasshopper.

unburied: Aeneas reigned only three years and his body was swept away by the river Numicus. The rest of her curse involves the adventures of Aeneas in Books VII-XII, with a reference to the Punic wars. The "avenger" is meant to be Hannibal, the famous Carthaginian general.

PROSERPINA: (Greek name was Persephone) Pluto's queen in the underworld was supposed to cut the thread of life of women. The lock of hair refers to the custom of taking a few hairs from a victim before it was sacrificed. The dying were considered offerings to the gods of the underworld, and a similar rite was usually performed.

DIS: another name for Pluto.

SUMMARY: Book I opened with a storm of nature, symbolizing the many storms in Rome's future, eventually subdued by Augustus. Book IV, showing poetic continuity, concerns the storm of man's greatest emotion, love. In this book Virgil is perhaps farthest from Homer. The theme of men attracted to women is barely suggested in Homer. Hector bids a touching farewell to Andromache. Achilles sulks because Agamemnon stole his captive princess. Odysseus leaves Calypso, Circe, and Nausicaa, but no tragedy is involved. It is Virgil who has the "humanity" to elevate the deserted woman to the position of a heroine of tragedy. His conception of love as a tragic force is what makes him a timeless poet, with appeal even in this modern day. We see the suffering of Dido torn between the desires of the heart and the need for self respect and greatness. We see Aeneas facing the forces of passion, bearing their pain, and finally conquering them. Throughout the book runs the theme of the double conflict: the historical one between Rome and Carthage, hinted at in Book I in the opposing goddesses, Venus and Juno; and the human one. In the sense that Book IV stresses the struggle between personal happiness and heroic glory, between passion and control, it can be thought of as the climax of the whole poem.

BOOK V

The flames of Dido's funeral pyre cause a glow to spread over the sky which the fleeing Trojans cannot help but see. Everyone is filled with a sense of doom. To increase their downcast spirits a storm comes up and the chief helmsman, Palinurus, is not able to hold the course for Italy. The head winds are too strong. He advises Aeneas, however, that they can bear off and make for Sicily which is not too far distant. Aeneas gives his assent since the change of plan will enable him to visit his old friend Acestes. In addition, his father had died on Sicilian shores, so the island is doubly dear to him. Acestes, having seen the ships in the distance, is down on the shore to welcome the travelers when they land. The next morning Aeneas announces to everyone that it was a year ago that his father, Anchises, died. In his honor, he has decided to set the day apart for sacrificing and feasting. He also tells them that in nine days he will set up a great field day for sports. As he speaks, a snake slithers from behind the altar, winds its way among the sacrificial foods, tastes them, and disappears without hurting anyone. Holding it as a good omen, Aeneas finishes the sacrifice of two sheep, two pigs, and two heifers. Nine days later the sun rises in a cloudless sky and the Trojans and Sicilians gather together to take part in the sports.

The first contest is a boat race which turns out to be dreadfully tense. The captain of one boat, Gyas, pushes his helmsman, Menoetes, into the water for failing to carry out an order. While Gyas is taking over the helm, the other ships pass him. Sergestus is now in the lead but, rounding the mark (a rock which stuck out above the water) too close, his ship runs aground on a hidden ledge and all the oars on the port side are broken. Mnestheus, having prayed earnestly to Neptune, gleefully overtakes the foundering vessel. With only one more to pass he is certain of victory. The bows of the two ships are just about even, and it is Cloanthus' turn to pray. (He is the captain of the fourth vessel.) He promises a white bull to the sea nymphs, the Nereids, if they will help him. (For some reason they seem to have more power at this point than Neptune!) Cloanthus pulls ahead and is proclaimed victor. Crowned with a green garland of bay leaves he receives his prize, a cloak of purple embroidered with gold. The other three captains get prizes too, so no one's feelings are hurt.

> **COMMENT:** Virgil is following Homeric tradition in his "field day" in Book V. In Homer there are funeral games in honor of Patroclus (Iliad XXIII, 262 f.). However, the boat race is original with Virgil, as is the later riding exhibition. All the sports have one thing in common: the man least expected to win, wins!

NAMES AND PLACES

ERYX: son of Neptune and Venus; thus half-brother of Aeneas. He was king in Sicily.

ACESTES: Since Laomedon had refused to pay Neptune his wages for building Troy, the god sent a great sea-monster to which maidens were to be thrown as prey. One clever father sent his daughter, Segesta, to Sicily to avoid this doom. Acestes was her son.

snake: thought of as the guardian spirit of tombs. His seven coils stress the magic number seven.

PHAETHON: son of the Sun-god. He begged his father to let him drive the chariot of the Sun, and going too close to the earth in North Africa began to burn everything. In the passage, Virgil is using the name of the son to mean Apollo for poetic effect. A thunderbolt hurled Phaethon to earth and restored the sun.

MNESTHEUS, SERGESTUS, CLOANTHUS: Prominent Roman families of Virgil's time liked to think of themselves as having Trojan ancestors; the Memmians from Mnestheus, the Sergians from Sergestus, the Cluentians from Cloanthus.

PHORCUS: a son of Neptune and father of frightful beasts who had hissing serpents for hair, claws of brass, wings, and enormous teeth. They were called Gorgons.

PANOPEA: a sea nymph.

PORTUNUS: an Italian god of the harbors.

MELIBOEA: town in Thessaly famous for its purple dye.

(LINES 286-603.) Now follow three traditional sports: racing, boxing, and archery. The foot race is exciting because two very close friends take part, Nisus and Euryalus. Nisus is far ahead when he slips on a spot where the heifers had been killed for the sacrifice. But though he can not get up in time to keep the first place, he thinks of his friend who is third and manages to trip up the number two man, Salius. Euryalus wins, but Salius of course is mad at the foul play. To calm everyone, Aeneas gives him a lion's hide as a prize. Even Nisus gets a trophy, since Fortune was responsible for his fall. So he receives a shield Aeneas had captured from a Greek seven years before. The first prize, a horse with all its trappings, seems hardly interesting at all.

The boxing match takes place between a Trojan super-man, Dares, and the Sicilian champion, Entellus. In fact, Dares is so powerful looking that at first no one from the Sicilian ranks will fight with him. Entellus gets up reluctantly only after much urging from Acestes. To make the match more equal, Aeneas provides them both with gloves of the same weight. It is Entellus, although he is much older, who delivers the final punches. Having fallen once when his opponent dodged a blow, he almost goes berserk in eagerness to finish Dares off. But Aeneas calls a halt. To show off his mighty strength Entellus takes his <u>caestus</u> (a thong loaded with lead and wound around the hand as a sort of boxing glove) and in front of the spectators, beats out the brains of the bull he had won with one blow. Dares staggers down to the water, coughing out blood and broken teeth.

The archery contest comes as pleasant relief. Aeneas has a mast brought from one of the ships and set up at a distance. A live dove is hung from the top as the mark. The first arrow, narrowly missing the terrified bird, sticks firm in the mast. The second man's arrow cuts the cord which ties the bird, and off she flies. In the nick of time, the third contestant takes aim and wings the dove. This leaves Acestes, who had decided to compete in spite of his years, with nothing to shoot. So he lets fly an arrow into the heavens. Catching fire it vanishes with a trail of flames behind it, like a shooting star. The crowd is struck dumb with amazement, and Aeneas interprets the marvel as a sign showing that Acestes is the winner. His trophy is a huge embossed bowl which had belonged to Aeneas' own father, Anchises.

The last scheduled event is a horse show, put on by young Ascanius and his friends. The boys, divided into three companies of twelve each, file down the center of the arena, then wheel. Half the group goes one way, and half the other. On each side there are three groups of six, and these charge each other across the open field. When they are just about to meet, the captains give a signal, and they wheel again, pretending to flee. Performing many other skillfull maneuvres, the boys show off their horsemanship to the delight of their proud fathers. (Virgil is giving a mythological explanation for the Ludus Troiae, a sport revived by Augustus in his youth-fitness program.)

> **COMMENT:** The descriptions of the various sports are really quite vivid, though in some places they tend to be too long. The reader does wonder, however, where such an enormous number of prizes came from, especially if he knows anything about the tiny size of ancient ships! But it is important to notice the change that has taken place in Aeneas. He is the on-looker, the director, much more than the participant. Virgil calls him "father Aeneas" (pater), much more than he calls him "noble Aeneas" (pius).

NAMES AND PLACES

Olive crowns: the traditional prizes given at the Olympic games in Greece.
THRACIANS AND AMAZONS: were noted for their skill in archery.
shield: the trophy given to Salius had belonged to a Greek who had dedicated it to Neptune, and then taken it from the temple when he went to war.
PARIS: more famous as a prize-fighter than a warrior
AMYCUS: son of Neptune, king of the Bebryces (a mythical people in Bithinia) had world-wide renown as a boxer.
HERCULES: the most famous of mythological heroes, known especially for performing twelve impossible labors. He also boxed with Eryx (see above) and killed him. His grandfather was Alcaeus, from whom came the name Alcides.
ERYMANTHUS: mountain in Arcadia in Greece where the famous boar, which Hercules killed, lived.
CISSEUS: king of Thrace, father of Hecuba, Priam's wife.
LABYRINTH: according to legend, a winding maze of paths in Crete at the end of which was the half-bull, half-man beast kept by Minos the king of Crete. Modern excavation has uncovered a huge palace at Knossos with innumerable rooms and halls from which the ancient legend may have had its start.
CARPATHIAN SEA: between Crete and the island of Rhodes.

(LINES 604-871.) All of a sudden the happy events of the field day are inter-rupted by horrible news. The ships, hauled up on the beach, are burning. Not only that but the women, the very wives of the men participating in the sports, start the fire. Of course, it isn't completely their fault. Juno, the ever present enemy of the Trojans, is the source of the dreadful crime. She had sent her messenger, Iris, down to the women as they sat discontented by the deserted ships. Iris disguises herself as one of the Trojan women and runs around spreading more dissatisfaction. For seven years they have been chasing a fleeing Italy. Why shouldn't they settle down and build a new Troy right where they are? If the ships are destroyed, they will have to stay in Sicily; now is the time for action. She picks up a burning stick from the fire at the altar of Neptune, and throws it at one of the ships with all her strength. The women are taken completely by surprise. One of them points out to her friends that she who spoke is not the person she looks like. She is far too beautiful; she does not walk as a mortal walks. The goddess vanishes leaving a rainbow in the sky and all the women in a frenzy hurl sticks from the fire at the ships.

Ascanius, still in his mock armor, gallops down to the water's edge, followed by Aeneas and the crowd. Too late the women realize what they have done. Not all the water that the Trojans pour on has any effect on the fury of the blaze. Tearing his clothes in despair, pius Aeneas calls on Jupiter to save them, or else kill him then and there with his thunderbolt. Almost before the words are out of his mouth, a downpour comes. The half-burnt timbers are drenched and all but four boats are saved from the disaster. Up to now, Aeneas himself has not completely made up his mind what to do. He too, has been torn between Sicily and Italy. Now wise old Nautes comes to the hero with the suggestion that they leave all the unadventurous people who are too worn out to go any further, and go on to Italy without them. Those left behind can found their own city in Sicily.

That night, as Aeneas is weighing the pros and cons, his dead father appears in a vision. He tells Aeneas to follow the advice of Nautes and when he gets to the Italian shore near Avernus (where the ancients believed there was an entrance to the underworld) he was to let the Sibyl lead him to the lower regions where he, Anchises, would be waiting for him. There he would see the future revealed to him. So the next day everyone joins in marking out the site for the new Sicilian city of Acesta. After nine days of feasting and sacrificing, the time for sad farewells is at hand. Those who chose to stay behind watch the oars of the ships they might have been on, as the fleet pulls off into the distance.

Meanwhile Venus, on her guard because of Juno's latest trick, goes to Neptune to get a guarantee from him that nothing will go wrong this time. The king of the seas tells her she need not be afraid for her son any more. Only one man will die before the Trojans reach Avernus. Having said these words, he rides over the ocean, calming the heavy surf. Aeneas gives the order to crowd on sail and Palinurus sets the course for Italy. Poor Palinurus! Though he was completely innocent of any wrong to the gods or to his friends, Neptune had set his eye on him. Disguising himself as one of the Trojans, he approaches the steersman and offers to relieve him at the helm. But Palinurus, loyal to Aeneas as always, refuses. The god has not other choice but to make him fall asleep. Moments later he falls overboard. In spite of this calamity the ship seems to keep on her course for a few more hours as they make for the bay of Cumae (near modern Naples). When Aeneas finally realizes that the ship is drifting aimlessly he takes over the helm himself, stunned by his friend's loss.

COMMENT: In this passage, Aeneas, after one last moment of irresolution, turns decisively to his destined task. Although it had been made quite clear in Book III by Helenus that his new home was to be Italy, Aeneas kept wanting to take the easier path. First it was Carthage; then it was Sicily, but always at the moment of greatest trial one of the gods comes to his aid, either by jogging his memory, or else by enlisting the forces of nature on his side.

NAMES AND PLACES

DORYCLUS: brother of Pheneus, king of Thrace.
RHOETEUM: a rocky strip of coast along the Hellespont.
VULCAN: god of Fire.
NAUTES: beloved of Minerva because he brought the tiny wooden statue of the goddess, the Palladium, with him from Troy. The Nautii, a promi-

nent family during the days of the early Republic, claimed descent from
him.

ELYSIUM: according to Virgil, the portion of the lower world where the
heroes went after death. Tartarus is sometimes used to mean the whole
of the lower world, but here the reference is more probably to the section
where bad heroes lived in constant torture.

IDALIUM: town in Cyprus sacred to Venus.

LAURENTUM: an ancient town in Latium near the Tiber river.

PELEUS: king of the Myrmidons in Phthia in Thessaly, father of Achilles.
The reference is to Neptune's rescue of Aeneas when Achilles was after
him, as told by Homer in the Iliad, XX: 79-352.

GLAUCUS: a lesser sea-divinity, overgrown with shellfish and seaweed.

PALAEMON: son of Ino who was driven mad by Juno. She threw herself and
her son into the sea, and they were changed into sea-gods.

PHORCUS: another sea-god, sometimes called the "old man of the sea"
by Homer. (see earlier note in the chapter).

THETIS: mother of Achilles. The rest of the names are sea-nymphs
daughters of Nereus, as was Thetis herself.

LETHE: the river of forgetfulness in the underworld. The souls of the dead
drank of its water before they returned to the world to inhabit new bodies
and forgot their former life as mortals completely.

SIRENS: beautiful sea-nymphs who enticed sailors to destruction on their
rocks by their lovely songs. Virgil locates them near the bay of Naples.
After Ulysses tricked them, they drowned themselves. (Odyssey XII:
178-200.)

SUMMARY: Although at times the reader feels that Virgil leans a little
heavily on Homeric tradition when he inserted the descriptions of the funeral
games, most of them are tense little dramas on their own. This is especially
true of the boat race. The whole book is necessary for understanding the
growth of Aeneas' character. It also shows Virgil's belief that the divine
plays a crucial role in man's life.

BOOK VI

(LINES 1-235.) At long last the Trojan exiles reach the shores of Italy. The eager adventurers leap ashore to explore, but Aeneas heads for the higher ground where there is the temple of Apollo. Near by is the cave of the Sibyl who is Apollo's prophetess. On the gates of the temple are beautiful sculptures representing the legends of Crete. Aeneas and some of his friends stop to look at the gates, but are called away by the Sibyl who senses that the power of the god is going to come upon her. The Trojans must be ready to hear her prophecy. Suddenly she falls into a trance; her breath comes quickly; tremors shake her body. Her last coherent words are a command to Aeneas to make his prayer to Apollo before the moment passes. Aeneas prays for a revelation from the oracle and promises to build a temple of solid marble to the god and to establish a festival in his honor. The priestess sways more wildly, and then abruptly is still. From her lips comes the gloomy prophecy: for the Trojans more war, more bloodshed, and Juno's continued hatred, all because of another foreign bride (the first was Helen stolen by Paris). All these he must face more boldly than ever, and from a Greek city will come the first sign of safety.

Aeneas answers that after all he has been through, there is no form of struggle or danger he can not face. He begs her only to show him how to get to the underworld to see his father. She answers that it is quite easy to get down to the underworld, but very few manage to make it up again, unless they are under the special protection of Jupiter. First he must find the golden branch which Proserpina, the queen of the lower regions likes so much. If he finds it and can break it off easily, he will know fortune is with him. But he must bury the body of a friend who has died without his knowing it. Then he may try the road to the underworld.   *Polinurus*

Aeneas and his friend, Achates, leave the gloomy cave. Walking along the beach they are filled with dark thoughts. Suddenly they see a corpse on the ground in front of them. It is the bugler, Misenus, who drowned when they were seeking the oracle from the Sibyl. With many tears, Aeneas and his friends set to work to build the funeral pyre. All the while they are cutting down the trees Aeneas is praying in his heart for a sign of the golden branch. Then he sees two doves, the messengers of his mother, Venus, and is filled with joy. They lead him to the mouth of the cave of Avernus and suddenly settle on a tree. There the gold branch shone out, as yellow mistletoe does in winter. Effortlessly Aeneas breaks it off and carries it to the Sibyl. When the funeral pyre has burnt to the ground, the hero takes the urn with the ashes and buries it together with the dead man's armor, oar, and trumpet. Over everything he heaps a huge mound of earth. Only then is he free to make his way to the underworld.

> **COMMENT:** This book starts out on a mysterious and awsome note with its use of the words "cave", "hidden", and "gloomy". It also has many divine revelations, the first of which occurs in this passage. Lastly, it is full of symbolism. The sculptures on the gate of Apollo's temple recall the murals on the temple of Juno in Carthage. And throughout the book there runs a deep religious undercurrent: Aeneas' prayer to Apollo, the Sibyl's prophecy, and the funeral of Misenus are but foretastes.

NAMES AND PLACES

<u>DAEDALUS:</u>   the designer of the labyrinth, the den of the Minotaur, half-bull, half-man, for king Minos in Crete. When he incurred Minos' anger he fled from the island on wings which he had made and landed at Cumae.

<u>ANDROGEOS:</u>   son of Minos went to Athens to take part in the games in honor of Athena. When he had won every contest, the king of Athens, Aegeus, set him to fight the wild bull of Marathon, which killed him. In consequence Minos imposed a tribute from the Athenians of seven boys and seven girls to be sent every year for the Minotaur to eat. The son of the Athenian king, Theseus, finally brought an end to this tribute by killing the Minotaur. Ariadne, Minos' daughter helped him by giving him a ball of string which he unwound as he made his way into the labyrinth, and rewound to find his way out again. She went with the Athenians as they escaped from Crete, but was later abandoned on the way on the island of Naxos.

<u>PASIPHAË:</u>   wife of Minos, and also mother of the Minotaur.

<u>ICARUS:</u>   son of Daedalus who left Crete with his father. He flew too close to the sun so that the wax on his wings melted and he fell into the sea.

<u>CECROPS:</u>   the mythical founder of Athens.

<u>TRIVIA:</u>   a name for Diana because she was worshiped at the place where three roads (<u>tres viae</u>) crossed.

<u>AEACUS:</u>   ancestor of Achilles. Apollo guided the arrow which Paris shot and by which Achilles died.

another <u>ACHILLES:</u>   the king of the land Aeneas must conquer in Italy in order to found his city. His name is Turnus.

<u>GRAECIAN city:</u>   the city of Pallantium, ruled by Evander, who came from Greece. Aeneas goes to Evander for aid. Pallantium was on the Pallatine hill, one of the seven hills of Rome.

<u>ACHERON:</u>   a river of the underworld whose overflow was thought to form Lake Avernus and the marshy region around it. Even today there are sulphuric fumes and other signs of volcanic action in this area.

<u>ORPHEUS:</u>   a musician-poet of mythology who descended into the lower world to get back his wife Eurydice. He played so beautifully on his lyre that his wish was granted on condition that he not look back at her till they reached earth. At the last minute he turned around to make sure she was following, and so lost her forever.

<u>CASTOR and POLLUX:</u>   half-brothers who loved each other dearly. Their mother was Leda. Castor's father was Tyndareus, king of Sparta and father of Helen. Jupiter was the father of Pollux, which made Pollux immortal. Both were conceived the same night and so were twins. When Castor was killed Pollux was desperate with grief. Finally Jupiter allowed the twins to take turns sharing life. Each spent one day in the underworld and the next day with the gods.

<u>THESEUS:</u>   went to the underworld to rescue Proserpina who had been carried off from her mother, Ceres, by the king of the lower regions, Pluto, whose other name was Dis.

<u>ALCEUS:</u>   grandfather of Hercules whose last labor was to bring up from the underworld the three-headed dog, Cerberus.

<u>COCYTUS:</u>   one of the rivers that bounded the Lower World. It was the river of wailing and a tributary of the Acheron, river of woe.

<u>MISENUS:</u>   Virgil incorporates part of an early legend which dealt with the death of a comrade named Misenus. To this day a cape at one end of the bay of Naples bears his name.

(LINES 235-627.) Into the dark, damp, smelly cave Aeneas goes. There he and the Sibyl perform ritual sacrifices to the gods of the lower regions. Then, as the sun rises, the earth rumbles with the threat of the volcano. The Sibyl shrieks at the Trojans to get out quickly. Aeneas she commands to unsheathe his sword and follow her. Down they go, through gloomy, ghostly passages. In front of the gates of the underworld they come upon Grief, Care, Disease, Old age, Fear, Famine, Poverty, Death, Misfortune, Sleep, Guilty Conscience, War, and Strife. They are enough to panic any man! Other monsters, Harpies and Gorgons seem to come at the hero, and he is about to slash at them with his sword but the Sibyl prevents him. They are only ghosts. They come to the bank of the river Acheron. Crowds of men and women, boys and girls are standing at the river's edge, begging the hideous ferryman, Charon, to take them across. Bewildered, Aeneas asks his guide what is happening. She tells him that all the people trying to get over the river are the unburied dead. Charon can not take them across until they have been given a proper funeral and their ashes are covered with earth. Only after they have wandered back and forth for a hundred years can Charon take them. Aeneas looks at them again with great pity. Going further, Aeneas finds several of his drowned companions and among them Palinurus, the faithful helmsman. He implores Aeneas to at least perform the ritual of throwing three handfuls of dirt on his corpse so that his spirit may have rest, or perhaps to take him back to the upper world. The Sibyl scolds him for trying to change the laws of heaven, but gives him one consolation. The people living along the coast near where his body was thought to have been washed up will build his tomb and name the promotory after him. They leave Palinurus a little cheered up and start to board Charon's boat. At first he refuses to take them, because earlier mortals whom he ferried over had all sorts of bad schemes up their sleeves. The Sibyl assures Charon that Aeneas is not going to carry off the underworld queen, as did Theseus, or do any other trick. As proof she holds out the golden branch which had been hidden under her robe. Charon is appeased, and ferries them over.

On the other side, the monster dog, Cerberus, snarls menacingly. To him the Sibyl throws a cake made of honey and sleep-inducing herbs. The dog promptly falls asleep and Aeneas enters the gate it had been guarding. The terrible wailing of new-born babies who died almost at birth, the moaning of suicides and unhappy lovers, meets their ears. It is here that Aeneas comes upon angry Dido. He tries in vain to gain her understanding and forgiveness, for her grief is more than he can bear. His explanation that it was the decree of the gods which forced him to leave her fails completely to soften her anger. Keeping her eyes on the ground and without changing her expression at all, she walks away. The great hero can not keep back the tears.

On and on Aeneas and the Sibyl go through the half-light. Soon they find themselves surrounded by famous Trojan heroes who are delighted to see Aeneas and want to talk with him. Among them is the son of Priam, Deiphobus, whose body is so mutilated that Aeneas barely recognizes him. He tells the hero the story of his horrible death and Aeneas would have stayed with him longer, if the Sibyl had not reminded him that soon the time would be up. He must not forget that the main purpose of his coming was to see his father, Anchises. So they come to where the path divides. The right fork leads to the Elysian fields where they will find Anchises. The left leads to the dungeon of the damned with its massive gates. These souls must atone for the crimes they commited on earth. Rhadamanthus is their harsh judge. At each stroke of the whip which the goddess of vengeance, Tisiphone, wields a scream of anguish rends the air. Aeneas, with horrified fascination, looks back as he and the Sibyl set off on the path toward the Elysian fields. The Sibyl describes some of the punishments. The giant Tityos is condemned to having his liver forever eaten by a vulture. Ixion and Pirithoüs live under the constant threat of a rockslide from a mountain falling on them, while just beyond their reach is a table laden with delectable things to eat. (This punishment is usually assigned to Tantalus. Ixion's punishment is usually a fiery wheel and Pirithous is chained to a rock. Virgil changes the legend.) The Titans who tried to overthrow Jupiter are condemned to eternal torture. Phlegyas, who burned the temple of Apollo at Delphi, speaks out his grim warning: "Learn justice, and do not despise the gods."

> **COMMENT:** This long central section gives Virgil a chance for two things. 1.) He shows his tremendous knowledge of myths and superstition. Yet the stories of the heroes and heroines are carefully worked in to create an atmosphere of gloom and horror. The nobility and glory of Anchises' prophecy in the last section of the book is heightened by the tremendous contrast with the murky terror of the middle part. 2.) The poet puts a spotlight on the humanity and compassion of Aeneas. The meeting with Dido, and Deiphobus, the looking back are put in purposely to stress these qualities. For Virgil understanding the sufferings of others is part of the process of becoming a hero.

NAMES AND PLACES

EUMENIDES: a nice sounding name for the Furies, the goddesses of vengeance. It meant "well-wishers." The most famous were Tisiphone, Allecto (whom we meet in Book VII) and Megaera. Their mother was Night. Earth was Night's sister.

STYGIAN KING: Pluto.

PHLEGETHON: river of fire in the underworld.

CENTAURS: a wild race living on Mt. Pelion in Thessaly. They delighted in bull-killing, and according to most legends, were thought to be half man, half horse.

BRIAREUS: a giant with a hundred hands.

LERNA: a marsh in southern Greece where the water-serpent, Hydra lived. She was killed by Hercules in the second of his twelve labors.

CHIMAERA: a fire-breathing monster with the head of a lion, the tail of a dragon, and a goat's body .

GERYON: a giant with three bodies, slain by Hercules.

VELIA: a Greek town not far from modern Naples.

PIRITHOÜS: friend of Theseus, and originator of the idea of carrying off Proserpina.

AMPHRYSUS: a river in Thessaly where Apollo tended the flocks of the king, Admetus.

MINOS: king of Crete who became a judge in the underworld after his death. The other two judges were Rhadamanthus and Aeacus.

PHAEDRA: hanged herself because of her love for her stepson, Hippolytus.

PROCRIS: checking up on her husband to see if he was faithful to her when he went hunting one day, was shot accidentally by one of his arrows.

ERIPHYLE: after being bribed to convince her husband, Amphiaraus, to war against Thebes, was slain by her son. The husband was killed in the war.

EVADNE: jumped onto her husband's funeral pyre after he, likeAmphiaraus, was killed in the war against Thebes.

LAODAMIA: killed herself when her husband was slain at Troy.

CAENEUS: started out as a maiden, Caenis, but was changed into a boy by her lover Neptune. In the underworld she regained her feminine form.

MARPESSA: a mountain in Paros, the island famous for marble. Dido is pale and unmoved, like marble.

TYDEUS, PARTHENOPAEUS, ADRASTUS: legendary heroes of the war of the Seven Against Thebes, the most important war before the expedition against Troy. The next group are heroes of the Trojan war.

LACONIAN WOMAN: Helen, who married Deiphobus after his brother Paris was killed.

AEOLUS: (not the king of the winds) king of Thessaly, was not the father of Ulysses, to whom this passage refers. But it was said that his son, Sisyphus, was the father.

ALOEUS: his wife, Iphimedia, and her lover, Neptune, had two sons, Otus and Ephialtes, who are generally called the sons of Aloeus. Their crime was trying to reach heaven by piling Ossa on Olympus, and Pelion on Ossa. (All three are mountains in Thessaly.)

SALMONEUS: king of Elis (southwestern Greece) who scornfully imitated the thunder and lightning of Zeus.

LAPITHS: a tribe in Thessaly ruled by Pirithoüs, son of Ixion, whose bride was affronted by one of the Centaurs. Thus arose the famous struggle between the Lapiths and the Centaurs. (The most well-known portrayal of this battle was a frieze on the temple of Zeus at Olympia.

(LINES 628-901.) At long last the gruesome journey nears its end. The hero and his aged guide reach the archway that opens onto the Elysian fields. At the entrance Aeneas sprinkles his body with water for purification, and plants the golden branch. Here is ''the joyful land, the pleasant grassy spots, the happy abodes of the blessed groves.'' The atmosphere is purer, filled with a rosy glow. In such an enchanted place no one is miserable. Some take part in sports, others dance; Orpheus plays his lyre. The ancestors of the Trojans are there with their phantom horses and chariots. The good priests, the noblest poets, philosophers and scientists who have benefited mankind crowd around the two visitors from the upper world. The Sibyl asks the tall poet in the center of the group, Musaeus, (he was considered a father of poetry) where they can find Anchises. He shows them the way, over the ridge and down into the next valley. There Anchises is retelling the story of his race and their descendants. Tears spring to his eyes at the sight of his son as he runs toward him with outstretched arms. How long he has waited for him to come. Aeneas struggles vainly to embrace his father, but only clasps air. If he cannot touch him, at least he can ask questions. Seeing a large number of people clustered round the river Lethe in the distance, he asks who they are. They seem like a swarm of bees hovering around luscious white lilies in the summer. His father tells him that they are the lucky souls who are given a second chance at life. But first they must drink the waters of forgetfulness. Aeneas is filled with pity at the thought of so many souls longing for the light of earth again. Anchises realizes that his son does not fully understand and so gives him a lengthy explanation of the philosophy of the transmigration of souls. After men die, even those who are good, their souls are still contaminated by having been incased in mortal bodies. So in the underworld the soul must pay the penalty till the taint is washed away. At the end of the cycle of a thousand years, when the soul is completely pure again, it is ready to go back to earth and live in a new mortal body. The last thing they do is to drink of the river Lethe so that they will forget what their former life on earth was like.

At the end of this philosophic explanation Anchises leads his son to a rise of ground from which all the people waiting to go to earth can clearly be seen. Then, with ever mounting pride, he points out Aeneas' son, grandson, and descendants who will raise the glory of his line to the stars. Of those nearest in line to the front, the most famous is Romulus, who was to found Rome. Off to one side stands Numa, the second king of Rome, who was the author of her religious customs. Beyond him are the other kings, warring Tullus, boastful Ancus Marcius, and the three Etruscan kings, Tarquin, Servius Tullius, and Tarquin the Proud. The heroes of the early Republic come next: Brutus, who deposed the last king of Rome, Tarquin the Proud, and many others. Down the centuries Anchises traces the men who are to make Rome great. There are also the men responsible for the terrible years of civil war and among them Caesar and Pompey. In another group are those whose victories in war helped the spread of empire. With them are the great men who defeated the power of Carthage. But at the end of the line there stands a soul greater than all. He is Caesar Augustus. Under him the long lost Golden Age will return again to Italy. The wonderful order of his rule will extend even to the stars. There is virtually no end to the glorious array of Rome's heroes.

And the blessings Rome will give to mankind cannot be matched. Others may create more life-like sculpture, may be more clever orators, or wiser astronomers. "Your destiny, oh Roman, is to govern the peoples of the world with order, to plant in them the habit of peace, to spare the conquered, and to crush the proud."

But Anchises has not quite finished naming the souls when Aeneas sees a young man of great beauty with melancholy eyes, and wonders who he is. He is the young Marcellus whom Augustus adopted as his successor. All Rome loved him, but he died prematurely at the age of twenty. His great promise came to nothing. Never was there such a funeral, or such mourning. Anchises finishes speaking, and leads his son through the rest of the realm of the Elysian fields. Finally Aeneas takes his leave, his spirit fired with passion for renown. Through the gate of Sleep which was for false dreams, the hero and the prophetess make their way. Soon Aeneas is back with his friends. The sail north to Latium is short. "Anchors are cast from the bows; the sterns rest upon the shore."

> **COMMENT:** This final section of Book VI resounds with the majesty of Rome's greatness. This is because the idea of the mission of Rome was almost a religion with Virgil. His creed is expressed in the stirring words toward the end of Anchises' speech: order, peace, mercy, justice, these were to be Rome's gifts to mankind. This magnificent revelation of Rome's destiny completely fills Aeneas. From this point on he consciously connects his mission with the future of Rome. The memory of his past fades before the hope of his future. The man has truly become the hero.

NAMES AND PLACES

CYCLOPS: one-eyed monsters who forged the iron for the walls of Pluto's palace.

ERIDANUS: the river Po flows underground for about two miles near its source which was why the ancients thought it rose in the underworld.

TITANIAN STAR: sun. Many ancient philosophies (the most famous being the Stoic) held that the primary cause of life and motion was a sort of world-soul which had a nature like that of fire.

PROCAS, CAPYS, NUMITOR, SILVIUS AENEAS: traditional kings of Alba Longa.

NOMENTUM ETC.; old Latin towns near Rome.

ROMULUS: son of Ilia (Rhea Silvia, daughter of Numitor) and Mars. According to legend, he was the founder of Rome in 753 B.C.

BERECYNTIA: mountain in Phrygia sacred to Cybele, the Great Mother. She was represented as wearing a crown of towers.

SATURN: expelled from heaven by Jupiter, ruled Italy in the first Golden Age, when all was peace and happiness.

GARAMANTES: a tribe from the interior of Africa to which was sent an expedition in the time of Augustus.

INDUS: here Virgil is referring to the east in general, by naming a prominent river there.

MAEOTIA: in southern Russia, area around the Sea of Azov.

LIBER: the early Italian god of fertility, connected by the Romans with Bacchus. In the legend Bacchus' chariot, drawn by tigers, went as far as India. (Nysa is a mountain in the Punjab area of India.)

CURES: a town of the Sabines, birthplace of Numa Pompilius.

FASCES: rods (for whipping) and an axe which were carried in front of the highest officer as a symbol of power (imperium). At first they were the exclusive right of the kings, but after Brutus they were taken over by the consuls. When Brutus' sons conspired to restore the king to power, he put them to death.

DECII: three generations of this family fought for Rome in the battles with the Latins, Samnites, and Pyrrhus respectively. (The Latin war ended in 340 B.C., the Samnite in 290, and the war with Pyrrhus, from Epirus on the north-west coast of Greece, 280.)

DRUSI: a good Roman family, but not famous for any great deeds. They are mentioned as a compliment to Augustus because his wife, Livia, was of that family.

TORQUATUS: killed his son for disobeying orders in war.

CAMILLUS: after he had been exiled from Rome on false charges he was recalled to defeat the conquering Gauls, (around 390 B.C.) All these stories would be familiar to every educated Roman.

MONOECUS: modern Monaco, one of Julius Caesar's strongholds. His daughter, Julia, was Pompey's third wife. After her death in 54 B.C. reconciliation between the two rivals was no longer possible. Most of Caesar's army came from Gaul, while Pompey recruited his from the eastern portion of the Mediterranean. Caesar claimed descent from Venus, through Aeneas, and thus was proclaimed a god after his death.

CORINTH: destroyed by Mummius in 146 B.C.

AEACUS' son: here refers to Perseus, the last king of Macedon, who was defeated by Aemelius Paulus at the battle of Pydna in 168 B.C.

CATO: known as the censor for his stern conservatism. He was most famous for the words he always repeated before the Senate: "Carthage must be destroyed," and was thus in some ways responsible for the start of the third Punic War.

COSSUS: an early Republican hero.

GRACCHI: brothers, Tiberius was tribune and murdered in 133 B.C., Gaius in 121. Both tried to bring about reforms so that the common people would have a greater voice in government.

SCIPIOS: a family famous for two hundred years of Republican history. The ones mentioned here are probably the two "Africani." Africanus the elder won the battle of Zama in 202 B.C. which ended the second Punic War. Africanus the younger destroyed Carthage in 146 B.C. at the end of the third Punic War.

FABRICIUS: rejected the bribes of Pyrrhus, 278 B.C., and later defeated him.

SERRANUS: nickname of Regulus, a general in the first Punic War. It comes from the latin word meaning to plant seed. The messengers who brought him the news that he had been elected consul found him planting in the fields.

MAXIMUS: His whole name was Quintus Fabius Maximus Cunctator (the last name means the Delayer). Since the Carthagian general Hannibal seemed impossible to beat, Fabius refused to meet him in a pitched battle. Instead he harried him in the rear and finally wore him out.

MARCELLUS: consul 222 B.C. killed the chief of the Insubrian Gauls. He is mentioned for the purpose of adding glory to his namesake, Marcellus. The second Marcellus was the son of Augustus' sister Octavia. He married in 25 B.C. the emperor's daughter, Julia, and was adopted by Augustus as his heir.

CAIETA: town in Latium which got its name from being the burial place of Aeneas' old nurse, Caieta.

SUMMARY:
Book VI may seem to imitate Homer's tale of Ulysses' journey to the underworld (Odyssey, XI, 2-332), but actually it has a far grander scope.

1.   Although there are many passages which are distinct echoes of Ulysses' experiences, (such as when he tries to embrace the spirit of his mother, but she, like a shadow or dream, flits out of his grasp) the weird, solemn, and philosophic mood is wholly Virgilian. Ulysses meets heroes and talks to them, but he is neither affected nor changed by what he sees. Aeneas, on the other hand, can not help feeling pity for the sufferings of the unhappy souls he meets, and he changes from wavering and being insecure to possessing heroic spiritual strength.

2.   The whole narrative is interwoven with symbolism. The theme of this symbolism is the relation of the world of myth to the world of history. Both worlds are controlled by Jupiter who represents order. Violators of world order suffer eternal punishment (such as the Titans who tried to overthrow Jupiter's rule). The theme of the interrelation of myth and history is not only a theme of book VI, but also a central idea of the whole Aeneid. However, Virgil expresses it most clearly in the religious and philosophic atmosphere of this book. (It is possible that Virgil also thought of the journey through the underworld as symbolic of the tragedy of life.)

3.   The third theme which transcends the simple narrative of the Odyssey is the glory of Rome, the theme with which the book closes. In the sense that the Aeneid is written to show the symbolic relation of history and myth to glorify Rome, book VI contains the essence of the whole poem.

BOOK VII

(LINES 1-284.) At the end of the last book Aeneas sets sail from Caieta. Book VII starts with the explanation for the harbor's name. Aeneas' nurse, Caieta, dies there, and the Trojans do not sail till they have completed the funeral rites for her. It is late afternoon when they finally get under way. Soon a full clear moon rises, casting its sparkling path of light upon the water. As the fleet sails northward it passes so close to the realm of the enchantress, Circe, that the Trojans can hear the howls of the men she has changed into lions, bears, wolves and other wild beasts. But Neptune is on guard and takes care to send favoring winds to speed them by the dangerous spot. As dawn comes up, Aeneas makes out the foaming mouth of the Tiber off to starboard, and gives the order to change course. They sail into the mouth of the peaceful river.

This land is ruled by king Latinus. Both he and his wife, Amata, are getting old, and have no son to inherit the kingdom. Their only child is a girl, Lavinia, whose hand is sought in marriage by all the neighboring princes. Of these the most renowned in valor and war-like deeds is Turnus, the young king of the Rutulians. The queen is anxious for Lavinia to marry this eligible suitor but, unfortunately, there are numerous oracles and omens which seem to be against the union. The most dreadful of these omens occurred when Lavinia and her father were sacrificing at the altar and the princess' hair caught on fire. When Latinus went to the oracle of his father, Faunus, to inquire the meaning, he was told that his daughter was destined to marry a foreigner, and that their descendants would bring eternal glory to his name. It wasn't long before Rumor had spread the story of the oracle throughout the surrounding countryside. By the time Aeneas lands everyone knows about it.

The travelers beach their ships and prepare something to eat. They make flat round cakes of cornmeal, on top of which they place the wild fruits they have gathered. It can hardly be called a banquet. In their hunger they eat the tasteless cakes too. All at once Iulus speaks up, almost without thinking: they are eating their tables. An awed hush falls over everyone as they remember the Harpy's prophecy. (Aeneas seems to have forgotten that it was the Harpy who made the prophecy, and says that he remembers his father, Anchises, saying the words.) In any case they consider it a good omen and Aeneas makes a special prayer to his father, and to the guardian spirit of the spot. The wine bowls are filled again and again.

The next day comes the task of building the city. One hundred chosen men go with Iulus as envoys to king Latinus. The rest remain with Aeneas to start work on the foundations. Iulus' embassy is impressed with the life and vigor of Latinus' city and eagerly seeks an audience with the king. When they see the carved images of Latinus' ancestors before the door to the temple they realize from what a long line and noble race he descends. The old king greets them graciously, and asks them whether a storm drove them to his shores, or whether they have strayed from their course. The spokesman for the Trojans, Ilioneus, steps forward and explains that they came to his land on purpose, as it was decreed by fate. He adds that they hope to settle, since they have been exiled so long from Troy, and to build their own city. Promising to be loyal allies, he offers Latinus relics which were saved from burning Troy: the golden bowl with which Priam poured libations at the altar, his sceptre, and his crown. Latinus is deeply moved by the gifts, but even more by the thought that these Trojans may be the foreigners to whom the oracle referred; their leader may be his daughter's fated husband. So he gives them permission to settle, but asks especially that Aeneas come in person that he may welcome him. The embassy receives a parting present of three hundred horses with purple and gold trappings. For Aeneas there is a chariot with two beautifully matched horses. The future looks rosy indeed.

> **COMMENT:** The most important aspect of this passage is the atmosphere of peace and friendship which pervades every line. All the events are favorable to the Trojans. Virgil has taken great pains to create this tranquil mood to heighten the contrast with the rest of the book.

NAMES AND PLACES

CIRCE: an enchantress who lured men to her island and then changed them into beasts. She was the daughter of the Sun and her horses were immortal. Ulysses in his adventures managed to outwit her (see Odyssey, X).

ERATO: the muse of love poetry.

TYRRHENIAN BAND: another name for the Tuscans, a people living in Italy, who revolted against their tyrant Mezentius and joined Aeneas.

FAUNUS: father of Latinus, son of Picus, and grandson of Saturn. He was worshipped as the god of the fields and of oracles.

ALBUNEA: a sulphurous spring.

NUMICIUS: a small river in Latium flowing into the Tyrrhenian Sea.

ITALUS: an ancient god from whom the name Italy was thought to come.

QUIRINUS: another name for Romulus, the first king of Rome and the first religious diviner.

AURUNCI: an early primitive tribe in Latium.

CORYTHUS: an Italian hero, son of Jupiter, father of Iasius and Dardanus.

(LINES 285-571.) Just when things seem to be going smoothly for everyone, Juno comes along. The sight of Aeneas and his friends rejoicing and building their city fills her with rage. In spite of all her efforts, storms at sea or marriage to Dido, the Trojans have managed to make it to Italy. Other gods have been able to take vengeance on those they hated, but she, the wife of the ruler of the universe is foiled at every turn. If the Olympian gods will not give her her way, the she will try the powers of the underworld. Although she is well aware that she can not change the decree of Fate (that Aeneas will wed Lavinia), at least she can put it off as long as possible. The goddess of war (Bellona) will be Lavinia's bridesmaid. To bring to pass these vindictive thoughts Juno summons the Fury, Allecto, from the underworld. She begs this hellish creature, dripping with snakes, to stir up strife and hate among Latinus' people: "Sow the wicked seeds of war."

How diabolically Allecto carries out the command! First she seeks out the queen mother, Amata, who wants Turnus for her son-in-law, in spite of her husband and the oracles. Standing over the queen with her hideous snakey tresses, Allecto takes one of the vipers hanging around her neck and thrusts it under a fold of Amata's robe. The queen is unaware of what is happening, but she grows more and more frenzied as the poison from the snake runs through her veins. At last the thought of her frustrated plans drives her wild, and she roams ranting and raving from one end of the city to the other calling on the other mothers to hear her wrongs. Only Bacchus is worthy to be her daughter's husband. Allecto drives her on, like boys driving a spinning top with their sticks, and all the Latin women are roused.

Having done as much harm as she could in that direction Allecto hastens to Turnus' palace. The young king of the Rutulians is peacefully sleeping...but not for long. The fiendish Allecto transforms herself into an aged priestess of Juno and appears to him in a dream. She tries to arouse his jealousy by taunting him that he is letting a foreigner walk off with his bride without a fight. All he has to do is to burn the Trojan's ships, kill their leaders, and Lavinia will be his. Turnus answers that he is well aware of what is going on but that it is not her business. She is supposed to attend to her sacrifices. Allecto, stung by these words, blazes with fiery anger. In the dream she changes back to her horrid form and the hissing of her innumerable snakes fills Turnus with terror. She hurls a torch at him and, sweating with agony, he starts from his sleep crying for arms. His whole spirit seethes with passion for war, the way a huge kettle boils fiercely when more and more wood is piled on the fire. He calls all the Rutulians to the defense of Italy.

Now Allecto turns to the Trojans. Her prey is young Iulus who has gone hunting, but her attack is directed at the hunting dogs. She fills them with madness for the scent of a stag which turns out to be no ordinary stag but the pet of the royal herdsman's daughter. Iulus takes true aim and hits the animal, but it manages to limp home. The daughter, wringing her hands in distress, calls upon her neighbors to help her find the villain who did such a wretched deed. The result is a pitched battle and the drawn swords glint in the sun as do the white crests of the waves, ruffled by an ever-increasing wind. Blood flows on both sides and even the man who tries to make peace is killed. So Allecto returns to Juno in haughty triumph and points with pride to what she has achieved. If Juno will say the word she will spread the war even further. The queen of the gods, however, is a little fearful of the horrible Fury and tells her she has done enough. Anything more that needs to be done, she, Juno, can see to. Flying away on her hissing wings Allecto returns to the underworld.

> **COMMENT:** This is one of the most artistically conceived passages in the _Aeneid._ The anger of Juno is mild beside the frenzy of Allecto. The pitch of the Fury's frenzy grows more intense with each visitation. The increasing insanity of Amata gives way before the terrible violence of Turnus' dream. This violence is in turn surpassed by the ferocious eagerness of battle. And dominating each scene is Allecto, a symbol of the demonic force of the historical world. What a contrast to the tranquility with which the book opened!

NAMES AND PLACES

INACHUS: river near Argos, named for the first king and most ancient hero of Argos.

PACHYNUM: south-east promontory of Sicily. The gods were supposed to visit their favorite spots once a year, and in this passage Juno is going from Argos to Carthage.

SIGEUM: the northwestern promontory in Asia Minor at the entrance of the Hellespont.

CALYDON: a town in Aetolia in Greece famed for the wild boar which inhabited the nearby mountains. The goddess Diana sent the boar to ravage the town because its king, Oeneus, had failed to sarifice to her. (Iliad, IX,533 ff.)

MARS: not the starter of the battle between Lapiths and Centaurs, but thought of as the destroyer because he was the god of war.

CISSEUS: a Thracian king, father of Hecuba, who dreamed before her son Paris was born that she would give birth to a burning torch. Juno says that Venus also has produced a torch because her son Aeneas will bring ruin on the new Troy by marrying Lavinia, as Paris did on old Troy by marrying Helen.

PHRYGIAN SHEPHERD: Paris.

ACRISIUS: a king of Argos whose daughter, Danaë, went to Italy, and married Pilumnus, an ancestor of Turnus. Ardea was the name of their city.

TRIVIA'S LAKE: modern Lago di Nemi where there was a grove of Diana.

NAR: a river famed for its sulphurous waters which flowed into the Tiber.

VELINUS: a lake some seventy miles north-east from the Trojan camp.

AMPSANCTUS: a lake east of Naples which gave forth poisonous odors. It was therefore thought of as one of the entrances to the underworld.

(LINES 572-817.) Once the battle has begun, there is no stopping it. As the wounded and the dead are brought home their wives and mothers cry for vengeance. Only Latinus resists the mass hysteria, and when he sees that his will has no effect among the people he resigns his rule. Hiding away he refuses to open the gates of the temple of Janus because that would be an official declaration of war. So the goddess who caused the war, Juno, comes down from Olympus to perform this act. With what eagerness do the people prepare for war! New forges are opened up so that more arms can be made. Even the horses seem proud to be going to war. All Italy blossoms with armed men.

The list of warriors is long and awesome. First there is the Tuscan, Mezentius, the scorner of the gods, with his handsome son, Lausus. Next comes Aventinus, son of Hercules and Rhea, striding along on foot, and swinging a terrifying lion skin. After him are the twins, Catillus and Coras, grandsons of a king of Argos, Amphiaraus. Then follows the king and founder of Praeneste, Caeculus, with his strangely armed battalion of slingers wearing helmets of wolf-skin. Next Messapus parades by accompanied by mail-clad warriors lustily singing marching songs. Then there is Clausus the Sabine with a host of Latin allies, and Halaesus, another man born in Argos and therefore eternal enemy of the Trojans. The tenth leader is aged Oebalus whose men use poisonous darts for weapons. A half barbarous tribe from the mountains led by Ufens comes next, and after them the priest, Umbro. He is sent by Archippus, king of the Marsi. Then Virbius, the son of exiled Hippolytus, (see below under names and places for his story) drives his horses and chariot over the plain.

At last Turnus appears, taller by a head than any of the other leaders. On his helmet is that most dreadful of fire-breathing beasts, a chimaera (lion-goat-dragon combination). His shield is emblazoned with a picture of Io being changed into a heifer. (She was the daughter of Inachus, the first king of Argos. Jupiter loved her, but she was changed into a heifer because of Juno's jealousy.) Rank on rank of armed infantry follow him.

Last of all the warrior maiden Camilla leads her troop of horse. As she goes by, the wives and mothers stare at her in amazement. Forward they all go to war; Turnus and his allies are prepared.

> **COMMENT:** Virgil gives this catalogue of warriors for two reasons: one is in deference to Homer's catalogue of ships (Iliad, II, 484 ff.) The other is to give a feeling of buildup toward a frightful war. Juno, as always, stands as the symbol of the unleashed passion involved in fighting. It is important to notice that most of the Italian allies are only half civilized, in contrast to the followers of Aeneas.

NAMES AND PLACES

GETAE: a tribe living near the mouth of the Danube conquered about 25 B.C. Virgil is praising the exploits of Augustus. Arabs in the next sentence refers to an expedition in 24 B.C.

HYRCANIA: a province north-east of Persia inhabited by Parthians. The standards which the Parthians had conquered from Crassus in 53 B.C. were restored to the Romans in 20 B.C.

GABINE CINCTURE: a ceremonial manner of binding the toga so that it became shorter and closer around the body.

HELICON: a range of mountains near the Corinthian Gulf in Boeotia, sacred to Apollo and the Muses. Virgil invokes the muse before his catalogue of warriors as Homer does before the catalogue of ships.

GERYON: a three-headed monster, living on the island Erythea, near Gades, Spain. Hercules managed to steal his beautiful oxen. Tirynthian is an epithet of Hercules because he was brought up in Tiryns.

SABELLI: lesser tribe of the Sabines.

TIBUR: a town not far from Rome, said to have gotten its name from Tiburtus, one of the three grandsons of Amphiaraus. It's modern name is Tivoli.

HOMOLE AND OTHRYS: mountains in Thessaly.

GABII: an early Latin town not far from Rome. The legend of Caeculus' birth was that his mother was sitting by the fire and a spark jumped out and thus she conceived by Vulcan, but abandoned the child near the temple of Jupiter after it had been born.

ANAGNIA: the largest town of the Hernici about thirty-six miles east of Rome.

AMASENUS: the god of the river of the same name located in Latium.

FESCENNIUM, CAPENA, MT. SORACTE: all located in Etruria, north of Rome. Mt. Ciminus is west of Soracte. The Falisci inhabited a town near Fescennium.

ASIAN POND: refers to the valley of the mouth of the Cayster river in Asia Minor, a favorite haunt of swans.

QUIRITES: inhabitants of Cures, a Sabine town; also the 'Men of Quirinus'.

AMITERNUM: another Sabine town. The next group of names all refer to either towns or rivers or mountains in the Sabine territory.

HERMUS: a river in Asia Minor, flowing through Phrygia and Lydia.

LYCIA: a southern district in Asia Minor.

MASSICUS: a mountain in Campania near the frontiers of Latium, famous for its wine.

SIDICINI: a Campanian tribe.

CALES: a Campanian town.

SATICULA: town north of Capua.

SEBETHIS: a nymph who lived in a small stream near Naples. Oebalus was not satisfied with his small kingdom of Caprea (Capri) and extended it to the north. The Teleboae were a pirate tribe who settled in Caprea.

ANGITIA: a goddess worshiped by the Marsi.

FUCINUS: a lake in central Italy about fifty miles east of Rome.

HIPPOLYTUS: son of Theseus. His step-mother Phaedra fell in love with him, but he rejected her. In anger she accused him falsely to Theseus who had his son dragged to death by horses. Later, when he discovered Hippolytus' innocence, Diana persuaded the god of healing, Aesclepius, to restore his body. His name was changed to Virbius, and he was placed under the protection of the nymph Egeria, in the grove of Aricia.

SICANI: a tribe Virgil indentifies with the Siculi who first inhabited Latium and then spread south into Sicily.

SACRANI: a mythical people.

LABICUM: an ancient town in Latium.

ANXUR: early name for Tarracina, a town southeast of Rome.

FERONIA: an old Italian deity worshiped in Etruria and the Sabine region, goddess of fields and fertility, and freedom from slavery.

SATURA: a marshy lake in Latium, formed by the Ufens and the Amasenus rivers.

VOLSCI: one of the tribes in Latium living to the south-east of Rome.

SUMMARY: Book VII begins what is commonly termed the "Iliad half" of the Aeneid. The first six books are considered the "Odyssey half." Virgil thought of it as parallel to Book I, but its development is directly reverse: Book I proceeds out of the violent storm at sea to the peace of Dido's court. Book VII goes from the tranquil Tibur setting at sunrise to the tumult of war. Allecto symbolizes the cruel power of the historical world as the storm is the cruel force of the natural world. The contrast between peace at the beginning and war at the end of the book is emphasized because of Virgil's own hatred of war, especially civil war. The whole book is permeated with the spirit of Allecto, the terrible personification of the unleashed passion of battle.

BOOK VIII

(LINES 1-369.) Turnus has raised aloft the signal to arm, and from all over Italy men flock to his standard. Aeneas is only too well aware of this. Full of uncertainties about fighting against such great odds, he walks back and forth along the edge of the Tiber. As night falls he lies down to rest, and out of the fog of the river a figure seems to rise and take the shape of the god of the river itself, Tiberinus. The kindly gray-haired old man speaks encouragingly to him, telling him not to dread the coming war. He promises him a good omen when he wakes up: Aeneas will see a white pig with a litter of thirty young around her, and they too will be white. This will be a sign that in thirty years Aeneas' son, Ascanius (also called Iulus), will build the city, Alba Longa. All that is necessary now is to find some allies. Further up the river is the city of Pallantium, named after king Evander's grandfather, Pallas. Evander is constantly at war with the Latin people and is sure to welcome Aeneas as an ally. With a parting warning to sacrifice to Juno so that her anger may be appeased, the river god disappears into the mists from which he rose.

Getting up from the damp ground Aeneas looks around and sees that dawn is approaching. He is considerably heartened, however, by his vision and promises to remember the nymphs of the place and Tiberinus in his sacrifices from this day on. Then he hurries off to get two ships ready for the voyage upstream. As they are about to shove off, Aeneas notices a white pig and her brood on the bank. The promised omen! The hero catches the pig and performs a solemn sacrifice to Juno.

Then, greatly cheered, the Trojans bend willingly to the oars. For a day and a night and half the next day they row without resting, till they see in the distance the towers of Pallantium. As they make ready to beach their boats the young son of Evander, Pallas (who has come down to the river to participate in a festival in honor of Hercules), spies them, and demands to know who they are. Aeneas, holding out an olive branch as a sign that they have come in peace, tells him that they are Trojans, and hostile to the Latins. He asks Pallas to tell Evander that they have come to seek an alliance. Pallas is delighted with this information and the two go off arm in arm to find Evander.

Aeneas' first words remind Evander that they are distantly related, and that though the king's ancestors are Greek and his Trojan, they should be friends. Evander looks at Aeneas for a long time without speaking. Then his face brightens with a flash of recognition. How like his father Anchises he looks! Gladly he welcomes an alliance with the son of so noble a father. But before they can talk business, the festival of Hercules must be celebrated. Aeneas is invited to participate and the celebration starts off with a great feast. While they are eating, Evander tells him the reason for their veneration of Hercules. This famous hero had saved them from the terrible monster, Cacus, who had terrified their countryside with his plundering. When he stole some of Hercules' prize cattle he went too far and was finally caught and strangled. From that time on they have set aside one day a year in his honor. The festivities continue with dancing and singing tales of Hercules' great deeds. There is more food, and more wine and, after a final prayer, they return to the city. As they go, Evander fills Aeneas' ears with stories of the early days of the region and of the various kings who reigned. In the city itself he points out the important historical monuments. Finally they reach the Tarpeian hill (later called the Capitoline). There is a definite feeling of awe about its wooded summit, and all the peasants believe that some unknown god lives there. In reality, this early settlement, which Evander thinks of as a city, is little more than a primitive village. On the level ground at the foot of the hill, destined one day to be the great Roman forum, cattle are grazing. Evander's palace is only a hut. The bed he offers to his guest is made of leaves, its sheets are of bearskin. None the less, the great Hercules himself slept under the same roof, and Aeneas, though born to the luxury of a Trojan prince, does not scorn the humble home of this simple Italian king.

COMMENT: This passage symbolizes Aeneas' introduction to the customs and religious observances of Italy. It is only by leaving behind forever his Trojan ways that he can become a true ancestor of the Romans.

NAMES AND PLACES

<u>DIOMEDE:</u>   an old enemy of Troy who colonized Argyripa, or Arpi, in Italy.

<u>PALLAS:</u>   a king in Arcadia in Greece. His city was Pallantium, and his grandson Evander used the same name for the city he founded on the Tiber in Italy. Pallantium was later incorporated into Rome.

<u>AMPHITRYON:</u>   supposed father of Hercules. He was the husband of Alcmene who bore Hercules by Jupiter in the guise of Amphitryon.

<u>ATLAS:</u>   one of the Titans who rebelled against Jupiter and was forced to bear the world on his shoulder. He is the common ancestor of Evander and Aeneas through his two daughters, Maia and Electra.

<u>DAUNUS:</u>   king of Apulia and father of Turnus.

<u>GERYON:</u>   a monster living in Spain. After Hercules slew him, he carried off his cattle and went to Italy. It was these same cattle that Cacus stole. The worship of Hercules was originally a family worship of the Potitia and Pinaria clans.

<u>SALII:</u>   dancing priests, usually associated with religious festivals to Mars. Here they take part in the worship of Hercules.

<u>TROY AND OECHALIA:</u>   captured by Hercules, the first because Laomedon refused to give him his reward for killing a sea-monster; the second, a town in Thessaly, because its king, Eurytus, refused to give him his daughter Iole.

<u>EURYSTHEUS:</u>   king of Argos, for whom Hercules performed the twelve labors. Juno hated Hercules, as she did most of Jupiter's children who weren't her own also.

<u>HYLAEUS AND PHOLUS:</u>   centaurs.

<u>CRETAN MONSTER:</u>   the bull which legend says he brought back alive to Eurystheus. All these are references to some of the twelve labors. He strangled the Nemean lion, carried back Cerberus, three-headed dog guarding the entrance to the underworld, and burned off the nine heads of the Lernian Hydra.

<u>TYPHOEUS:</u>   frightful beast with a hundred heads, hands and eyes.

<u>CARMENTIS:</u>   mother of Evander and a prophetess.

<u>ASYLUM:</u>   built by Romulus to house refugees and thus increase the population of Rome. It was supposed to have been located between the two summits of the Capitoline hill.

LUPERCAL: a cave under the western side of the Pallatine hill, connected with the worship of Lupercus, an Italian god of the country.

LYCAEUS: a mountain in Arcadia where Pan, the Greek god of shepherds and flocks was born.

CARINAE: name of a wealthy section of Rome.

(LINES 370-731.)   While Aeneas sleeps on his crude bed and all Italy is wrapped in darkness, Venus, his loving mother, begins to be concerned with the preparations for war. She decides to use her beautiful charms on Vulcan, the god of fire and forges, to persuade him to make the armor for her son. In the past he made arms for Achilles at his mother's, Thetis', request, and she, Venus, has not asked him for a single favor before this. She caresses him enticingly, kisses him, and his resistance vanishes. He promises to forge the strongest shield imaginable. Bright and early the next morning he departs for Sicily where the mighty forges of the Cyclops glow. There the smiths were working on a thunderbolt for Jupiter, and making a chariot for Mars. Vulcan tells them to stop everything and get to work on Aeneas' armor. At the same time that work on the shield begins, Evander and Aeneas get to work arranging the alliance. The king has the brilliant idea of enlisting the aid of the cities of Etruria which have revolted against the cruelties of their king, Mezentius. Hated for his murders and tortures (such as tying living bodies to a dead one, and letting them die in misery), he was finally driven out to seek refuge with his friend Turnus. Evander assures his guest that the Etruscans will willingly join him, not only because of wanting to kill Mezentius, but because an oracle has told them that a foreigner will come to lead them. In addition to the Etruscan army, Aeneas can have a token force led by Pallas, Evander's son, for to the old king, there is no one better suited for showing his son the arts of war. The treaty is on the verge of being settled when, in the cloudless sky, there is a tremendous clap of thunder. The hero looks up and thinks he sees arms flashing red in the blue air.   Joyfully he tells his host that the thunder is a sure sign from his mother, Venus, that she is bringing the armor which she promised. Hastily Aeneas sacrifices to the guardian Lar of Evander's home, and then runs off to tell the rest of his men what has happened. A group of the best fighters he picks out to stay with him; the rest he sends back to his son, Ascanius, so that he may make proper preparations.

At this point, rumor of the approach of an advance Etruscan delegation reaches Pallantium. Aeneas decides to go and treat with them. As part of the embassy, Evander sends his son, Pallas, with a moving prayer to Jupiter for his safe return. Whatever happens, he wishes to die before he should hear news of his only son's death. With a mighty fanfare they set off for the Etruscan camp, and Pallas in the middle is seen to shine with the beauty of the Morning star.

As the delegation enters a wooded region, close to where the Etruscans are camped, Venus approaches, holding out the arms Vulcan has made. Mother and son embrace fondly, and then Aeneas turns to have a look at his exquisite armor. Never has he seen anything like it in his life. He fingers the thick plumes of the helmet with admiration, picks up the sword, trying it out for weight and balance. How well the ruddy colored bronze corselet fits him. How like the sun it shines! Even the greaves for his legs are crusted with gold. But more beautiful than all these is the fabulous shield. With infinite pains Vulcan had hammered into its surface scenes of Rome's future. Slowly, slowly, Aeneas turns the beautiful work of art around in his hands. His eyes pass over the picture of the wolf, which was to be the foster mother of the twins, Romulus and Remus. Next in order is the story of the Sabine women, carried off to be Roman wives. Then there is a picture of the king of the Sabines, Tatius, and Romulus, making peace. Here Horatius at the bridge is trying to prevent the Etruscans under Lars Porsenna from taking over Rome again. Then there is Manlius keeping the Gauls from the Capitoline after the hissing of the sacred geese had awakened him. There are scenes with Rome's enemies suffering in the underworld. In the very center is portrayed the glorious battle of Actium where the noble Roman, Augustus, conquers the oriental playboy, Antony. In the scene Augustus and his commander-in-chief, Agrippa, lead the fleet. Just beyond, the ships of Antony and Cleopatra can be seen, fleeing from the battle. All the gods of war are present, Mars, Bellona, and Discord. Venus takes up arms against Minerva; the Egyptian god, Anubis (worshipped in the form of a dog) attacks Roman Neptune. Pale Cleopatra and the weeping Nile-god are there, and finally Augustus Caesar himself, parading in triumph through the streets of Rome. Then he is seen consecrating all the temples, for his empire now extends to the farthest corners of their world. Proudly Aeneas raises high for all to see and admire the magnificent shield of Rome's future glory.

> **COMMENT:** The description of the shield, the high point to which the book has been leading, comes directly from Homer's description of Achilles' shield (Iliad, XVIII, 478ff.). But there the similarity ends. With Virgil every scene is prophetic of Rome's history, while Homer describes the varied occupations of daily living. This points up the differences between the two poets. One writes to glorify a nation, the other, to glorify man.

NAMES AND PLACES

NEREUS: father of the sea-nymph, Thetis, mother of Achilles.
TITHONUS: husband of Aurora who asked Vulcan to make armor for her son Memnon.
LIPARA: largest of a group of islands northeast of Sicily.
LEMNOS: one of the larger islands in the Aegean, sacred to Vulcan because it was there that he landed when Jupiter hurled him from Olympus.
TEGEA: important city of Arcadia, in Greece.
MAEONIA: another name for Lydia where legend says the Etruscans originated.
CAERE: also called by the older name Agylla, an Etruscan town.
ROMULUS AND REMUS: after floating down the Tiber in a make-shift cradle (they were abandoned by their mother who was a Vestal virgin) were found by a she-wolf who took them to her cave and nursed them till a shepherd boy rescued them.
METTUS: leader of the Roman allies from Alba Longa. In a battle when he was supposed to help the Romans, he refused to join, and later as punishment for treachery he was torn apart by chariots driven in opposite directions.
TULLUS: third king of Rome who ordered Mettus' execution.
COCLES: refers to Horatius Cocles whose superhuman valor kept the whole Etruscan army under Lars Porsenna at bay on the other side of the bridge to Rome. Behind him the Romans destroyed the bridge. In the nick of time he jumped into the river and swam back to the Roman side and to safety.
CLOELIA: A Roman virgin sent as a hostage to Porsenna. She escaped and swam back across the Tiber, but the Romans sent her to Porsenna again. He was so impressed that he set her free, along with several other hostages.

CATALINE: conspired to overthrow the senate in 63 B.C.

ACTIUM: one of the most famous battles in Roman history, between Augustus, and Antony and Cleopatra, actually more of a naval battle than a land operation, fought off the Ambracian gulf on the northwest coast of Greece, September 2, 31 B.C.   There was no town on the shore, only a temple to Apollo.

SABAEANS: a tribe living in Arabia.

IAPYX: the west-northwest wind blowing off the south of Italy and thus favorable to those crossing to Greece.

TRIUMPH: in August 29 B.C. Augustus celebrated a triple triumph for victories in Dalmatia, Actium and Alexandria.

MULCIBER: another name for Vulcan.

LELEGES AND CARIANS: peoples in Asia Minor.

GELONI: a Scythian people living near the Black Sea and south Russia.

MORINI: a people dwelling on the coast of Gaul (France) opposite Britain.

DAHAE: lived on the southeastern borders of the Caspian Sea.

ARAXES: a river rising in Armenia and flowing into the Caspian. The force of its current was proverbial.

SUMMARY: The end of this book marks the end of the middle third of the poem. It closes with Aeneas lifting high the shield on which Roman history reaches its climax in the victory and triumph of Augustus. This symbolizes the fact that the hero has at last become mature enough to bear the destiny of Rome.

BOOK IX

(LINES 1-167.) War at last! While Aeneas is away his enemies attack, for Iris, Juno's messenger takes care to inform Turnus of the Trojan leader's absence. As she vanishes into the rosy mist he raises his hands to her in prayer. Then comes the call to arms. The river of warriors is compared to the Nile or the Ganges in its mighty tide. Far in the distance the Trojans see the black cloud of dust rising toward the sky. With frantic speed they hurry behind the solid shelter of the wall of their settlement. It would be far more glorious to stay and fight before the walls, but the parting words of Aeneas before he left on his mission of alliance were not at any cost to attempt a pitched engagement. On his return he would tackle single handedly the enemy's champion. So Turnus, the passionate fighter, comes galloping up on his beautiful white stallion with an advance guard of twenty men, taunting the Trojans for their cowardice. Dramatically he hurls a javelin straight up into the sky, and then prances back and forth in front of the Trojan walls. His wild eagerness to get at the Trojans is likened to a starving wolf padding back and forth outside a sheepfold, not knowing how to get in. At last an idea strikes the impatient warrior. If he sets fire to the ships, surely the cowards will run out to save them. His followers, inflamed by Turnus' fury, with one accord throw flaming pine torches at the unprotected fleet. Clouds of black smoke billow skyward.

The mother of Jupiter, Cybele (also known as Rhea) sees the smoke in alarm. It was from her favorite mountain side that the pine timbers the Trojans used for their ships came. Surely Jupiter can do something to save her precious trees! Jupiter scolds her gently for trying to change fate, and then promises to change the ships into sea-nymphs. The fire has burned the ships cables, and as they drift out into the river, the pointed beaks of the bows seem to dive under the ripples and emerge in the form of beautiful nymphs. The Rutulians are terrified by this awesome sight and the horses whinny in fright. Only Turnus is calm; and he interprets the omen to their advantage: it is the Trojans who should be afraid, for now they cannot possibly flee. The Rutulian allies far outnumber the hated foreigners, and not even Venus herself will be able to help them. He, Turnus, does not need any trick, such as the horse the Greeks made at Troy, to get inside this puny settlement. Nor will he attack at night, but in full day light. But since most of this day is gone, the Rutulians retire to their camp and leave Messapus to set up a blocade of the walls. Soon the twilight is pierced by a ring of light from a hundred circling camp fires. The first day of battle is over.

COMMENT: This passage serves to show us the character of Turnus. He is a hero no less than Aeneas, yet somehow doomed to tragedy. He represents passion in contrast to Aeneas' self-control in the last half of the Aeneid, as Dido did in the first half. But he still posseses the most essential qualities of a hero: beauty, noble birth, youth and courage. Before going into battle he faithfully performs the rites due the gods. All this heightens the tragedy of his passionate fury, which is continually illustrated by comparisons with wild animals. And always he is the source of the destructive element with his army.

NAMES AND PLACES

THAUMAS: son of Earth and Sea, and father of Iris.
DOTO AND GALATEA: sea-nymphs.

(LINES 168-502.) Behind the walls the Trojans stand guard, but their courage is at low ebb. Aeneas is far away, and how can a messenger get through the enemy's blockade? Yet in the dark night, unknown to the rest of their companions, two close friends are forming a plan. Nisus, who guards one of the gates whispers excitedly to Euryalus of his burning longing to perform a deed of valor. Maybe this longing is sent by a god, or maybe each man makes such a longing into a god. Whatever the reason, he cannot stand remaining idle behind the walls when it is so essential to get word to Aeneas. Euryalus is fired by the idea and insists on going along. At first Nisus is against it because of Euryalus' youth, but finally the younger friend wins him over, and they set off to lay their plan before Ascanius and the other Trojan leaders. Ascanius is deeply impressed by their daring as is Aletes, the wise old war counselor. In fact the latter can not keep back the tears as he places his trembling hands on their shoulders. Aletes begs the two to name whatever reward they would like, but Ascanius interrupts to promise them greater treasures than they can dream of: two silver goblets worked with gold, two tripods, two talents of gold (a fortune for those days, close to $15,000) a bowl that had belonged to Dido herself, and if Turnus should fall in battle, his own beautiful white horse would be added to the prize. Euryalus has but one request. He has decided to depart on this perilous undertaking without telling his mother, for she could not bear it. If fate should decree that he not return, let Ascanius comfort his bereaved mother. Such filial devotion brings the noble son of Aeneas to the verge of tears, and he promises that Euryalus' share of the reward will go to his mother, should something so dreadful happen. Then he fastens his own sword on the youth, while Nisus receives a protective lion skin from Mnestheus, and a helmet from Aletes. Accompanied by anxious prayers for their safety and the success of their mission, the two set off.

Everything goes according to plan, at first, that is. The night is moonless and they creep from shadow to shadow till they are in the very middle of the slumbering enemy. All around them are bodies stretched out on the ground, overcome with too much wine, or the weary excitement of the day, or both. No one is awake to see them. Burning with revenge, they go from body to body, piercing one through the belly, cutting off the head of another, more like a lion mangling his victims in a sheepfold, than two civilized human beings. Indeed, Euryalus becomes completely swept away by lust for more blood. But Nisus catches hold of himself, recollecting the sacred nature of their mission. Already the shadows are less dark, and the sky is graying with the coming dawn. They must go now, while there is still a chance of making it to Aeneas. The younger man can barely manage to tear himself away from such a triumph. With almost childlike eagerness, he puts on as much of the armor of the men he has slain as he can: the sword-belt of one, and the helmet with lovely waving plumes of another. Sadly he leaves behind all sorts of arms, gold and silver bowls, beautiful carpets, and other priceless treasures. But the shining helmet was to be his undoing, for as they head for the path by the river leading to Pallantium, a troop of three hundred horsemen bear down upon them as they seek to hide in the brush along the road. They are coming to Turnus with messages and help from king Latinus. Three-hundred against two are pretty frightful odds. Still if they can reach a little footpath off to the left, they may have a faint chance of avoiding being seen. But the leader of the horsemen, Vulcens, catches sight of something, the plume of the helmet, white in the uncertain shadows and cries out for them to halt.

Fear gets the better of wisdom and the friends flee in opposite directions. Euryalus, being younger and terribly inexperienced, quickly looses his way, doubles back on his tracks without knowing it, and is captured. Nisus has better luck in eluding his pursuers, and could have gotten away all together if his tremendous love for Euryalus had not made him turn around. Realizing that Euryalus is nowhere in sight, he retraces his steps toward the sound of the scuffle. He too is now lost, for what possibly can one man do against so many? It no longer matters. All that does matter is that Euryalus shall not die unavenged. Forming a prayer to Diana under his breath, he dodges from bush to bush ever closer, till he comes upon Vulcens, just as he is driving home his sword into Euryalus body. Two others has Nisus already slain in his search for Vulcens. Now it is Vulcens' turn! As Euryalus rolls over, lifeless, Nisus plunges his sword right through the skull of his friend's slayer. Seconds later he too is killed. The two, inseparable in life, are now together forever. But victory has its price. The mourning embassy from Latinus, carrying the body of their dead leader, enters the Rutulian camp, which is also filled with grief for the countless men slain by the hands of the two Trojans. Nor does news of such a slaughter remain unknown for long. For Turnus, with the cruelty inspired by war, lifts high on sharp pikes the two heads of the reckless Trojans. The grief-stricken mother of Euryalus is almost the first to hear the grim story. Inconsolably she attacks heaven with her cries of anguish. Her son is not only slain by the enemy, but she can not even have the headless corpse to bury with the honor due a hero. Just as she is about to jump off the wall into the thick of the enemy, two Trojans at Ascanius' command carry her back to her room unconscious.

> COMMENT: The Nisus and Euryalus story is one of the most vivid in the whole Aeneid, and also one of the most romantic, in the sense that friendship is idealized and exalted, at the expense of wisdom and prudence.

NAMES AND PLACES

HYRTACUS: married Priam's first wife, Arisba, when Priam married Hecuba.

ASSARACUS: a Trojan ancestor; his Lar would thus be considered the guardian deity of the whole Trojan race.

ARISBA: a town in Asia Minor which sent allies to Troy.

CREUSA: Ascanius' mother, Aeneas' first wife who died at Troy. (See Aeneid, II.)

(LINES 503-818.) Now the piercing notes of battle trumpet rend the air as with ever increasing force the Rutulians redouble the attack. Scaling ladders are set against the walls, only to be pushed back by the Trojans. All along the top of the wall the Trojans roll down great stones. But especially fierce is the fighting in front of the high tower on the wall of the settlement, as the defenders there have tremendous superiority in being so high. Their arrows have deadly effect among the Rutulians. Suddenly Turnus grabs a blazing torch and hurls it with almost superhuman strength at the wooden

structure.   Fanned by the wind it soon is nothing but a mass of flames.
Then it comes crashing to the ground.   Two of the Trojans are thrown
into the ranks of the enemy: Helenor is killed instantly, but Lycus, attempting
to scale the wall and reach the outstretched hands of his comrades, is torn
down by triumphant Turnus.   Again and again the Italian allies come on,
under their heavy round shields, one man right beside the next, the whole
formation looking like a giant tortoise.

In front of another part of the wall parades an insolent upstart, Numanus.
Giving himself airs because he has just married Turnus' younger sister,
he shouts all kinds of jibes at Ascanius: he mocks him because of his style
of clothes hinting that he can not be a man if he wears a helmet with ribbons
on it, and purple embroidered gowns; he and all the Trojans must be women
since they do not even dare come out and fight. The Italians breed a race
of men, toughening them in infancy by washing them in the ice-cold river,
teaching them to hunt, and to master every tool and weapon made of iron.
Trojans are only good for dancing; fighting is not for women! Ascanius can
stand it no longer, and vowing a steer to Jupiter once a year till he dies,
if the king of the gods will guide his arrow, he takes aim, and shoots the
proud boaster through the head. Cheers go up from the ranks of the Trojans!
But Apollo thinks that Ascanius is too young to be fighting the battles of
men, and leaving Olympus, disguised as the boy's old tutor, Butes, remarks
to him that his shot was fabulous, but there will be plenty of opportunity
for him to fight when he is older. The Trojans who are standing around
sense that a god spoke the words, and restrain Ascanius in his eagerness.
But the youth's feat fires the weary Trojans as they return to the fray.

At that moment, however, two foolhardy young men take it upon themselves
to open the gates and charge the Rutulians. This was the one thing they had
been strictly commanded not to do, and its results were nearly fatal to the
Trojans. For far from being able to rush out, they are immediately charged
by the outnumbering Rutulians. Turnus himself, fighting tirelessly in one
part of the battle, hastens to the breach. The Trojans fall back in terror
before the fire in his eyes and his death-dealing sword. The sound of falling
bodies is worse than the crash of a landslide sending boulders rumbling into
the sea. None can stand against the might of Turnus. The brilliance of
his armor reflecting the sunlight is almost blinding. The blood-red plumes
of his helmet make him seem twice as tall as he is. Finally Pandarus, a
tall man in his own right, ventures to take him on. With a calm smile on
his face, Turnus raises his sword and cleaves Pandarus' skull in half.
The valiant Trojan topples to the ground, the halves of his head dangling
weirdly.   The Trojans scatter in terror as Turnus advances. In fact, if
he had not been carried away by mad lust for killing, he could have opened
the gates of the settlement. The Trojans had closed them behind him when
he had far outdistanced the rest of the Rutulians. But victory has gone to
his head and he looks only for the next man to kill.

Finally the Trojan leaders in despair hold a war council, and Mnestheus,
the leader, shouts out stinging words to his men: are they going to let
one man, all alone against so many, go unscathed? Where is their courage,
their love for the gods and for Aeneas? These words turn the tide, and step
by step they press Turnus back toward the river like a lion hemmed in on
all sides by hostile spears.   Even so they suffer two setbacks until the
whole Trojan army is massed against the one mighty warrior. Only when
he is overwhelmed on all sides, when the rain of arrows and stones on his

helmet and shield becomes deafening, and the blood-red plumes of his helmet are cut in two, does the thought of flight occur to him. With a headlong leap, he plunges into the Tiber, armor and all, and escapes back to his army.

> **COMMENT:** The pace of battle in this passage moves almost faster than the poet. There is a horrible fascination in the bloody exploits of Turnus. Though he is the villain representing the demonic fury of battle and the cruelty of war, it is impossible not to admire him.

NAMES AND PLACES

CALLIOPE: muse of Epic poetry.
SYMAETHUS: located on the east coast of Sicily.
PALICI: twin gods of Sicily, sons of Jupiter and the nymph, Thalia, who was Vulcan's daughter.   They were worshipped in the neighborhood of Mt. Aetna.
DINDYMUS: a mountain in Phrygia, sacred to Cybele.
SARPEDON: prince from Lycia, ally of the Trojans, killed by Patroclus.

SUMMARY: This is the book of thundering war in which Turnus is the star. It is also the book of wild animal similes: the lion, the wolf, the eagle. We may wonder how Virgil, a poet of pathos and insight, with seemingly tender sensibilities, could write such bloody battle scenes. And some critics may argue that the scenes lack the vitality and primitive power of Homer. They are still full of tremendous realism, symbolic of the blood-stained pages of Rome's history. By showing the horrors of war, Virgil makes the strength and glory of the peace which Rome finally brought to the world, under Augustus, even greater.

BOOK X

(LINES 1-117.) Meanwhile on Olympus, Jupiter becomes very upset at the continued fighting and decides to call a council of the gods as he had commanded that the Trojans and Rutulians should be friends. Unfortunately, like so many councils, it accomplishes little more than giving the rival parties a chance to quarrel in public. Venus naturally blames the war on Turnus, broadly hinting that Jupiter's wife has had a great deal to do with it. Still, if her grandson Ascanius is spared, she will be satisfied. Juno retorts that it isn't her fault if Aeneas attempts to marry someone else's promised bride (Lavinia). Now was she to blame that the Trojan prince, Paris, carried off Sparta's princess, Helen. It wasn't her fault either that the Trojan war started in the first place. All the rest of the gods take sides, and the dispute goes from bad to worse. Finally in disgust, Jupiter throws up his hands, saying that he will take neither side. Whatever happens is in the hands of Fate.

> **COMMENT:** These opening lines in many ways seem to be an unnecessary imitation of Homer's council of the gods (Iliad, beginning of IV and VIII). The only result is that Jupiter says he will not interfere. The power of fate is above the power of the gods.

NAMES AND PLACES

ALPS: a reference to Hannibal's crossing in 218 B.C when he led the Carthaginian forces.

ARPI OR ARGYRIPA: town in Apulia in Italy, founded by Diomede who settled there after the Trojan war. He was the son of Tydeus and wounded Venus when she rescued Aeneas from him (Iliad V, 336).

AMATHUS: town in Cyprus beloved by Venus.

PILUMNUS: ancient Italian god.

VENILIA: a sea-nymph, mother of Turnus; sister of Amata, the wife of Latinus.

(LINES 118-660.) Back among mortals, the battle rages fiercely, and the sorely tried Trojans begin to loose hope. But unknown to them help is at hand, for Aeneas approaches. With him is the small force of Evander and the huge army of his Etruscan allies. All night long the ships have been speeding toward the beleaguered settlement. At the head of one division of the Etruscan army is Ocnus, whose native city, Mantua is the head of a league of twelve cities. (Virgil inserted this bit to glorify his own home town, which was Mantua.) Guided by the moonlight the men bend tirelessly to the oars. All at once the fleet is surrounded by beautiful sea-nymphs. They are the hero's old ships which Cybele had changed into sea-nymphs to save from being burned by Turnus. One of them, Cymodocea, wakes Aeneas from his brief rest to tell him what has happened to those he left behind and to warn him about Turnus. Then she and her nineteen sisters swim behind the boat so that they skim along twice as fast. Aeneas breathes a prayer of thanks to Cybele for this wonderful omen.

By daybreak they are in sight of the settlement. A shout of joy rises from the throats of the exhausted Trojans. Their beloved leader has returned. Strengthened by fresh hope, they fight back fiercely. But Turnus, with brilliant strategy, decides to abandon the attack on the walls and to defend the shore instead. If he prevents the reinforcements from landing, the Trojans are doomed. But he gets there too late to hinder the first of Aeneas' men. Some leap into the shallow water as it ebbs back from the beach, others take their turn scrambling down the gangplanks. On and on they come, Aeneas at their head. Against him, none can fight, and live. Aeneas uses up all his weapons so fast that he has to send his friend, Achates, back to the ships for more. And in another part of the battle his young ally, Pallas, is fighting just as nobly. Having met tremendously stiff opposition the force given by Evander starts to give way. But Pallas spurs them on with high words, and gallops into the thickest part of the fighting. Every enemy falls before him, and courage returns to his men. Nearer and nearer he gets to where his counterpart among the Rutulians, Lausus, is putting on an equally good show of bravery. Just as Pallas and Lausus are about to meet, however, Turnus comes riding up in his war chariot, claiming that he alone has the right to fight Pallas. Alas for Pallas! For all his noble nature he is no match for peerless Turnus. The two size each other up and Turnus attacks like a lion a bull. Pallas throws his spear first, praying to Hercules to make it go true. But though it does pierce the armor at the shoulder, Hercules is powerless to go against the decree of Fate. For this day of battle is Pallas' appointed day of death. The power behind Turnus' huge oak spear is far greater. Its tip penetrates the armor through to the heart. But Turnus, in honor of his noble adversary, does not mangle the corpse but takes only the beautifully worked sword belt as his spoil. With loving care his friends bear the dead hero's body from the field.

News of Pallas' death drives Aeneas to his wildest deeds. Left and right he cuts the Rutulians down. He grasps one wretch who begs for mercy by the plume of his helmet and, bending his head way back, runs his sword through his neck. His weapons are warm with ever fresh blood. He attacks two brothers who come riding up in their chariot, drawn by two white horses. The first he pierces through the groin as he is about to take aim with his spear and the Rutulian falls over onto the ground. His terrified brother begs Aeneas to spare him, but the raging hero hacks him in two. Everywhere he looks for Turnus, but the latter is nowhere to be found because Juno, fearing that Aeneas might kill her dear Turnus, begged Jupiter for permission to get Turnus out of the fight. Jupiter grudgingly consented, and so Juno invented a ghost to look like Aeneas. And this she causes to flit around the scene of battle, so that Turnus, on seeing what he thinks is Aeneas, pursues it far from the fighting, down to a waiting ship, which is also part of Juno's scheme. As Turnus is about to run the phantom through, it disappears before his eyes. Filled with shame because he will now be thought a coward, Turnus bitterly reproaches Jupiter for pulling such an unfair trick. Nor can he get back to the battle, for Juno has cut the ship's cable and he is far out to sea. The thought of the army which has followed him so faithfully fills him with despair. No wonder Aeneas can not find him.

COMMENT: In this book Aeneas is the star warrior, even as Turnus was in book IX. But here we also get a fine picture of Turnus' character. He is not just a proud, cruel killer. His heroic qualities show forth at their best when he refuses to rob the dead Pallas of more than his sword belt, and when despair comes upon him at the loss of his honor. That he was tricked makes his tragedy all the greater. There is tragedy in the death of Pallas too, because his noble nature seems to attract such a destiny.

NAMES AND PLACES

ORICUM: town in Illyria on the Greek coast. The district was famous for its turpentine, or terebinth, trees.

IDA: the figurehead of the ship is a replica of Mt. Ida with Cybele's lions at its base.

CHALYBES: a people of Pontus who lived near the shore of the Black Sea and were famous for their iron work.

CYCNUS: father of Cinyras and Cupavo, beloved of Phaethon. When the latter was destroyed by Jupiter, Cycnus' grief was so great that he was changed into a swan.

STRYMON: the river forming the boundary between Thrace and Macedonia.

SIRIUS: the dog-star whose ascendency in the late summer was associated with diseases of that dry and unhealthy time.

LICHAS: children who were saved alive from dead mothers were dedicated to Apollo as the god of healing (also the sun-god).

SWORD-BELT: worn over the shoulder. Pallas' was engraved with the story of the murder of the sons of Aegyptus by the daughters of Danaus.

(LINES 661-908.) But though Juno has dishonorably removed Turnus from the fight, Jupiter raises up another warrior from the ranks of the Rutulians, equally as fierce. This is Mezentius, the deposed king of Etruria, whose cruelty is well known through the land. Like a lion maddened with hunger which spies a stag, leaps upon it, and then crouches over the carcass, gloating, with gory fangs, so does Mezentius leap at the Trojans who come against him. And Aeneas, since Turnus has disappeared, seeing this terrible havoc in the Trojan ranks, goes after him. For this encounter, Mezentius is ready and eager. Proudly he tells his son, Lausus, who is fighting at his side, that he shall wear the armor of Aeneas as Mezentius' trophy of battle. He hurls a spear at Aeneas, but it glances off the hero's shield, and kills another. Aeneas in his turn hurls his, and Mezentius is hit in the groin. Lausus cries out in horror at the sight of blood gushing from his dear father. But the older man fights on, though painfully with slowly retreating steps. Then, before his father can stop him, young Lausus leaps between pursuer and pursued, protecting his father's withdrawal with his own shield. Nor are his blows light, but Aeneas fends them off till Lausus has spent all his energy.

Then, and only then does the Trojan leader press the attack. In an instant he buries his sword up to the hilt in the young man's body. At the sight of so young a man lying dead before him, an irrepressible groan escapes from the hero's lips, for the image of Ascanius fills his eyes. He can not take the youth's armor, his right as prize of victory. In deep compassion he helps Lausus' friends lift up the lifeless body so they can carry it off the field, wailing as they go. The sound of their cries reaches Mezentius as he nurses his wound by the Tiber, his breath coming in short painful gasps. With bitter words he curses himself for letting the son fight the father's battle. The death of his only child touches the cruel tyrant as nothing else could. Wild with grief he crawls to his feet and manages to pull himself up onto his horse. As the horse paws nervously at the strangely unbalanced weight on his back, Mezentius talks encouragingly to the poor beast in low tones. Then, charging back to the densest fighting, he calls loudly for Aeneas: "I come, about to die, but first I carry these as gifts." Javelin after javelin he hurls at the wary Trojan as he circles round him, but his strength wanes, and the weapons bounce off the shield harmlessly. Finally Aeneas, tired of waiting and turning round and round, strikes the horse a mighty blow on the head. The beast rears up, pitching off his rider, and then rolls over on top of him. Unsheathing his sword Aeneas makes ready to finish the Etruscan. Waiting only to hear his foe's last request that he be properly buried, since his own people hate him, Aeneas plunges the sword through his throat.

Mezentius

COMMENT: This passage gives a wonderful portrait of Mezentius, the hated tyrant of Etruria. He is compared to a barren crag that resists all the buffets of the storms, to a wild boar which no one dares face, to a lion leaping on a stag, to a whirlwind, and to a giant. In contrast to him is Aeneas, who seems to have lost the savage ways with which he fought in the first part of the book, for his treatment of Lausus shows his compassionate nature.

NAMES AND PLACES

VESULUS: one of the Italian Alps-Monte Viso, whence rose the Po river.
CORYTHUS: an Italian hero, father of Dardanus; also a city in Italy.
ORION: a giant huntsman changed into a constellation by Diana.

SUMMARY: Perhaps the true hero of book X is Fate, for neither Jupiter's calm detachment, nor Juno's passionate partisanship can change the outcome of the war. Pallas and Lausus, the noblest of the young men on each side must die, and Juno's spiriting Turnus away has only put off the day of his death, as well she knows. For a brief period Aeneas is almost a Homeric hero, caught up in the present by the madness of war. But when, at the death of Lausus, he thinks of his own son, his destiny and future come back to him, and he is filled with pity for the young life that is to know no future. Thus the book where Fate is the hero ends on a note of true pathos.

BOOK XI

(LINES 1-444.) Both sides have had enough of war. There are so many dead! Envoys from Turnus' camp come seeking a truce to bury their dead at the very moment when the Trojans are in the middle of the ceremony in honor of Pallas. Around the bier made of oak twigs (the oak was sacred to Jupiter) and arbutus shoots (or wild strawberry tree, famous for its shade) the Trojan women wail, their long hair unbound as a sign of mourning. Even in death he is still beautiful, like a violet that has been picked but has not yet wilted. Sorrowfully Aeneas covers the body with a priceless robe made by Dido herself of purple cloth worked with gold. Then the sad procession sets out for Pallanteum to return the corpse to Evander. Interrupted by the Rutulian envoys, the line of Trojan men and women comes to a halt while Aeneas talks courteously to the emissaries.

Gladly he grants the twelve days truce they seek, and would willingly end the war if he could: it was not of his seeking. One of the Rutulians, Drances, who has never been in favor of Turnus' war, promises to do all he can to smooth things out with Latinus and to bring about an alliance with Aeneas; let Turnus find an alliance somewhere else. With these words they depart, and the funeral procession continues on toward Pallanteum.

Long before it gets there, however, the news of his son's death reaches the ears of Evander. Rumor has flown on ahead, and as the Trojans get closer to the city they see a long line of Evander's citizens, carrying flickering torches, winding out to meet them. Stumbling at the head of the group is the old king himself, his face streaked with the tears bewailing the cruelty of fate. He falls prostrate on the bier moaning that life has no more meaning. All he wants are vengeance for Pallas and his own death.

All over the fields smoke from the countless funeral pyres rises toward the sky. Latins, Rutulians, Trojans, made allies by death as they can not be in life, mourn their dead.

An additional cause for grief then comes to Turnus: Diomede has refused to join with them. Even though he fought against the Trojans long ago, he wants no part of fighting them now. Aeneas is far too noble. In fact, Diomede suggests that rather than giving himself gifts to cement an alliance, they should be presented to the Trojan leader. King Latinus is more than ready to follow this suggestion. His kingdom is large enough for Trojans and Latins alike. Happily would he give them a tract of land to settle in or, if they wish to go elsewhere, timber to build new ships. Drances speaks out in favor of Latinus' proposal, in keeping with his promise to Aeneas. One and all, the Latins long for peace and if the king's daughter, Lavinia, is given in marriage then the peace will be certain.

But the thought of such a disgraceful peace is more than Turnus can bear. He jumps up from his seat at the council and taunts Drances for his honeyed words; always the talker and never the doer! There have been rumors that he is a coward. Well, they will see who is the real man, the one afraid to fight, or the one who seeks glory in war. For the sake of Italy and his ancestors he is prepared to die, if necessary. One sure ally they do have, the warrior queen Camilla.

COMMENT: The moving description of the funeral for Pallas in this passage shows how deeply Aeneas (and thus Virgil) was affected by the bitterness of war. Aeneas' sensitivity to tragedy at the beginning of the passage is in sharp contrast to Turnus' love of glory, whatever the cost.

NAMES AND PLACES

PARTHASIA: district in Arcadia in Greece where Evander came from.

TROPHY: a victor's trophy was usually the trunk of some tree decked with the armor of the man he killed.

DIOMEDE: went with eighty ships to the Trojan war, and was the bravest of the Greeks, next to Achilles. After the war he left Argos and was driven by a storm to the east coast of Italy. There legend says that he founded many cities, among them Argyripa, or Arpi.

IAPYGIA: part of Apulia in southeast Italy.

GARGANUS: a promontory on the east coast of Italy, the modern Gargano.

CAPHEREUS: a promontory in Euboea in Greece where the Greek ships were wrecked returning from Troy. Athena (Minerva) sent a storm and the king of Euboea, Nauplius, hung out false lights to guide the fleet onto the rocks.

PROTEUS: one tradition makes him king of Egypt, and thus Virgil means the eastern end of the Mediterranean. (See Odyssey, IV;81).

NEOPTOLEMUS: also called Pyrrhus, son of Achilles, killed at Delphi, and his kingdom in Epirus divided, part of it going to Helenus (see Aeneid III, 325 ff).

IDOMENEUS: king of Crete, and one of Helen's suitors (see Aeneid III, 122 ff).

LORD OF MYCENE: Agamemnon, killed by his wife Clytemnestra, who was urged to the deed by her lover Aegisthus.

CALYDON: ancestral home of Diomede in Aetolia in Greece.

(LINES 445-915.) Into the middle of this council, where there only seemed to be disagreement, a messenger runs to say that the Trojans are advancing with their Etruscan allies. This is the chance Turnus has been looking for. Ironically he asks the assembled group if they are going to sit quietly talking peace while their city is being invaded. In a flash the council chamber is empty. Only Latinus is still angry with himself that he had not taken steps at the beginning to unite his daughter with Aeneas. No good could come from this renewed fighting. His queen, Amata, and Lavinia, along with the crowd of women, go to the temple of Minerva to pray for victory. Other women, and boys too, make for the walls of the city to aid in defense, so thinned are the ranks of the Latins and Rutulians.

Turnus, glad for action at last, charges out the gate like a powerful stallion bursting from the imprisonment of his stall, who heads for the open pasture, neighing in wanton joy. The warrior maiden, Camilla, gallops to meet him, and suggests that he stay by the walls to guard the city while she and her Volscian cavalry engage the light-armed horse of Aeneas and the Etruscans. Turnus decides to let her face the cavalry while he goes and ambushes the infantry as they come through a narrow pass. He is full of admiration for Camilla, as well he might be: she was hardened to war from infancy. When her father, Metabus, was driven by the enemy from his city he took with him in his flight his baby daughter. Unable to swim the flooded river encumbered by the child, he tied her to the middle of his spear-shaft and hurled it across, plunging in and swimming over just in time to save her. Safely beyond the reach of his pursuers, he took over the care of the tiny baby himself, and fed her wild mare's milk. Her first playthings were a bow and arrows, and while still a small child she mastered the art of the slingshot. In men she showed no interest but worshipped only Diana, the virgin goddess. No wonder she is such a magnificent fighter.

The whole plain now bristles with the spear points glinting in the bright sun. Spuring their horses on, the two armies charge toward each other and then, abruptly, rein in barely a spear's throw apart. The sky is blackened with the shower of spears and arrows. But the Latins fall back and flee toward the city. Suddenly they wheel about and attack their pursuers, who are routed in their turn. So goes the ebb and flow of battle. In the heart of the fighting rides Camilla, one breast bare, wielding her battle-ax, and shooting arrows even in retreat. She is more than the equal of any Amazon, or even that most famous of Amazonian queens, Hippolyta. Many a Trojan bites the dust because of her faultless aim.

Just then as the Etruscans seem to be losing heart, their leader, Tarchon, goads them into action by saying that they are cowards to be defeated by a woman. Like lightning, like an eagle, he goes through the ranks killing right and left. The sight of such magnificent fighting inspires the young Etruscan Arruns to go after Camilla. As Camilla recklessly pursues a Trojan priest, Arruns stalks her, praying all the while to Apollo. Suddenly she raises her arm to throw the spear, but Arruns hurls his first, catching her unguarded with uplifted arm. And while the Etruscan, flushed with victory, looses his head and runs from the scene, the warrior maiden vainly tries to pull the spear out, but the barb has gone too deep. Just before she topples lifeless from her horse she gasps out a last message to her sister to tell Turnus what has happened. He must return and defend Laurentum.

With Camilla dead, the Latin cause is lost. It is not a Rutulian who slays Arruns in revenge, or a Volscian fighting maiden, but one of the handmaids of the goddess Diana, Opis, performs the deed. Forgotten by his comrades he lies in the dust, pierced by an arrow of the virgin goddess. When the news of the disaster reaches Turnus he abandons his ambush and speeds toward the doomed city. Minutes later Aeneas and his troops come through the unguarded pass. Only the coming of the night prevents the two armies from engaging. But the die is cast, and the next rise of the sun will bring the final outcome.

> **COMMENT:** In this passage Camilla seems to personify the bright aspect of war, even as Turnus is the cruel aspect. The description of Camilla and her cavalry is completely original with Virgil, and considered by many to be his best battle scene.

NAMES AND PLACES

PRIVERNUM: a city in Latium on the Amasenus river.
THERMODON: a river in Pontus, Asia Minor, in the homeland of the Amazons.
PENTHESILEA: another queen of the Amazons who fought on the side of the Trojans. She was killed by Achilles.
GORTYNIA: town in Macedonia.
SORACTE: mountain in Etruria where there was a temple to Apollo.

The rites consisted of walking barefoot through hot embers.

SUMMARY: This book leaves the reader almost breathless. It starts with the slow sad dignity of the funeral procession, and ends with the mad, headlong flight of the remnant of the Rutulian army and the massacre at the gates as they crowd upon one another in their panic to escape the Trojans. Like a bright flash of light, Camilla appears in the last section, pointing up the way Virgil was torn between the tragic bitterness of war in real life, and the shining glamor of war in myth.

BOOK XII

(LINES 1-613.) Turnus now is the only hope. Only through him can Laurentum be saved. Still believing in his mission to preserve the nations of Italy as they existed before the Trojans' arrival, he burns with the desire for revenge, and madness increases. Picture a lion of the African jungle, who becomes truly ferocious only when wounded by the hunters. Turnus' wound is to his pride, but the pain is just as terrible. He entreats king Latinus, with mounting impatience, to set up the agreement that he and Aeneas may contend for their countries' honor, and for victory, in single combat. But Latinus is still for appeasement. Why should he not make an end of war while Turnus is alive, if he is willing to become an ally of the Trojans with Turnus dead? But his attempt at appeasement only increases the warmonger's passion. If he must die, at least death will bring him fame. His loving mother, however, intrudes in an emotional outburst: he must not fight in single combat with terrible Aeneas, for, if he dies, she will kill herself. Beautiful Lavinia, too, adds her tears to those of his mother. Turnus is appalled at the scene they are making. Tears are no fit accompaniment for a hero going into battle! Paying no heed to anyone, he summons his beautiful white horses, dons his armor, picks up the sword that Vulcan made for him, and seizes his spear, all with the grim frenzy with which a bull prepares to attack a tree trunk.

At the same time Aeneas makes equal preparations, rejoicing in his heart that the war is to be settled by single combat. The two sides troop together to confirm the agreement and make it binding. On one side Rutulians, on the other, Trojans, are marshalled with great pomp. Turnus brandishes two spears as he stands in his war chariot, drawn by the matched white horses. On the Trojan side, Aeneas strides forward, wearing his god-made armor which shines with blinding brilliance. Each combatant comes to the altar and makes the proper sacrifice. Aeneas speaks out a mighty prayer, calling on Sun, Earth, Jupiter, Juno, Mars, and Floods and Fountains as witnesses. If Turnus wins, the Trojans will retreat to Evander's city. His son, Ascanius (Iulus) will leave the land forever. They will never reopen the war. But if Aeneas wins, the victorious Trojans will be merciful, not seeking to rule the conquered, but living together as equals. And the city they build shall be named after his father-in-law's daughter, Lavinia.

The compact seems sacred enough, but Juno is always afraid for her dear Turnus. She still wants to save him if she can. Leaving Olympus, she seeks out the nymph of a fountain nearby. Her name is Juturna, and she is a sister of Turnus. Jupiter was her lover at one time, but because of her relationship to Turnus, she is the only one of Jupiter's amours whom Juno does not hate. Juno explains that she is prevented by Jupiter from doing anything more to help Turnus, but perhaps Juturna can think of something. She can, and does. Assuming the disguise of a noble Rutulian, Camers, she spreads dissatisfaction among Turnus' followers. Latinus is in the middle of making his vow to the gods. He invokes Earth, Sea, Stars, Apollo and Diana, and the gods of the underworld. Then he places his hands upon the altar, and the two leaders sacrifice the sacred animals to make the treaty forever unbreakable. But Juturna is whispering among the Rutulians that it is disgraceful, since they outnumber the Trojans, for them to let one man do their fighting for them. Even if he dies he will become famous, but they will be slaves.

At this critical moment a flock of wild swans is seen in the sky attacking an eagle which is trying to carry off one of them. The sheer weight of their numbers finally overpowers the bird of prey, and dropping the swan, he flies away into the clouds. Immediately this is interpreted as an omen that they should attack the Trojans.

One of the Rutilians casts a spear at the opposite side, and a wild free-for-all begins. The hail of javelins, spears and arrows is deadly. The solemn treaty, only minutes old, is worthless, and Latinus flees in despair. Some take up charred or burning sticks from the altar fire to hurl in the face of the nearest emeny. Others bash their opponents with battle-axes. In the center of the chaos stands Aeneas, bare-headed, shouting, in the vain attempt to get himself heard, that they must remember the treaty. His voice cannot possibly carry over the din, and his frantic gestures only serve to call attention to where he is. In a flash, an arrow from an unknown bow hits him in the knee. The hero becomes a martyr for the sake of law and order. He limps from the battle with blood streaming down his leg, while Turnus' spirits rise in a sudden surge of new confidence. He is more fierce than the very god of war himself as his horses trample the wounded under foot and the knife-blades on his chariot wheels cut men into ribbons. Completely forgetting the treaty, he creates havoc over the whole plain.

Meanwhile Aeneas' friends are frantically trying to stem the flow of blood from his knee, with virtually no success. Aeneas, paying no attention to the pain, works away at the barb of the arrow, but it has gone too deep and will not come out. Even the doctor, Iapyx, with all his knowlege of herbs, gets nowhere. So Venus must take matters in hand herself, and having cut a stalk of a plant which grew in Crete and was known for its healing power, she dips it into the water Iapyx is using to cleanse the wound. Immediately the flow is staunched, and the arrowhead comes out easily. The old doctor knows that a god has performed the miracle, but Aeneas hardly notices in his impatience to get back to the fighting. Filled with rage at the breach of the treaty, he drives over the battlefield like a mighty hurricane, sweeping everything before him. Tirelessly he seeks Turnus. But Juturna is guiding her brother's horses, and whenever it seems that he and Aeneas may meet, she drives them in the other direction. Hours after Aeneas searches for Turnus, killing only when he has to, and sparing those who flee for their lives. On his side, however, Turnus lusts for more and more blood as he stacks the heads of those he has killed, dripping with gore, on his chariot.

At last Aeneas gives up the chase temporarily and turns his energies to the walls and the high tower of Laurentum. Urging his soldiers on by the well-worn phrase that Jupiter is on their side, and determining to wait no longer for Turnus, he leads them with one accord in wedge formation up to the walls. Fires break out in a hundred different places at once. Scaling ladders are thrown up, the guards at the gates are cut down, clouds of smoke billow higher and higher. Poor queen Amata, thinking that the city is completely in the hands of her enemies and that Turnus is already dead, hangs herself in despair. The city resounds with the howling of women.

COMMENT: The various battle scenes in this book tumble one upon the other with such ever increasing speed that it is hard to find a pause. Of the two major actors, it is Turnus who commands our attention the most. His role is similar to Dido's in the fourth book, for both are controlled by passion. In this first portion of the last book death stalks in every line, but destiny is continually put off. Slowly, slowly, Turnus looses his confidence, which is first shaken by the tears of Lavinia and his mother. He goes forth to battle, not so much to win, as to fight and die nobly. Of his own free will he chooses glorious death if necessary, but the breach of the truce and the interference of his sister, Juturna, prevent it. Still, the atmosphere of tragic apprehension mounts as the Trojans attack the walls in disciplined formation, while within the city, all is panic.

NAMES AND PLACES

AGYLLA: small Etruscan town.
DOLON: Trojan spy, killed by Diomede. (Iliad X: 314 ff.)
EDONI: a people living in Thrace on the Strymon river.
LYNISUS: a town in Asia Minor.

(LINES 614-952.) Far in the distance, Turnus faintly hears the cries from the doomed city, and he begins to loose his zest for fighting. Filled with anxiety he determines to go back and to find out what has happened. Juturna, in her disguise as his charioteer, urges him to stay and fight where he is. The more Trojans he kills, the more famous he will be. But Turnus' eyes are opened and he recognizes his sister, in spite of her disguise. Full of reproaches he asks her what right she has to interfere. His luck has run out and the only hope left is that he may be spared any more humiliation, all because of meddling goddesses! 'At least let me win glory by dying nobly.'

At that moment a wounded Rutilian, Saces, gallops up shot through the face by an arrow, but valiantly determined to perform his duty. Though his face is contracted by pain his words confirm Turnus' horrible suspicions: the city is on the verge of collapse; the queen has commited suicide.

The words are a dagger in Turnus' heart. In anger he orders his sister to be gone. He will meet Aeneas now, and banish the shame that hangs over his name already. She may call it madness if she likes. His mind is made up. Like boulders broken loose from the top of a mountain leveling everything in their path, Turnus charges toward the city. Exultantly Aeneas sees him coming and thunders out to meet him. The din of swords clashing on shields is deafening. Turnus raises his sword high for the great blow, but it strikes the god-made shield of Aeneas...and snaps in two. Turnus leaps back in horror, looking at the broken weapon. Only then does he realize that the sword is not his own but his charioteer's which he snatched up by mistake. His own sword, made by Vulcan, would not have failed. Wildly he searches first for his own sword and then calls to his men for one of theirs, as Aeneas pursues him round the circle made by terrified Trojans and Rutilians.

Then Aeneas hurls his spear but it misses its mark and sticks fast in a clump of wild olive saplings. Turnus, catching his breath in this unlooked for delay, breathes a prayer to Faunus, the guardian spirit of the olive, to hold the spear fast so that Aeneas may not be able to pull it out. And while Aeneas is tugging away with all his might, Juturna (still disguised as the charioteer) runs up to Turnus with his missing sword. Venus then gets angry that Juturna should have such power and comes down to free the spear for Aeneas. With the aid of the gods the odds are evened up again! Jupiter, too, ceases to be a spectator as he forbids Juno (for her power is behind Juturna's actions) to meddle any more: 'Is it not enough for her that she drove the Trojans over the sea, wrecked them on the shores of Carthage, and started this terrible war? What greater signs of power does she need, anyway? Juno must admit that he is right. And seeing that Turnus and his side are doomed she asks that the two sides become united under the Latin name and that the descendants be Romans, possessing the primitive strength of Italy. Let the name of Troy fall into oblivion. Jupiter promises that this wish shall be fulfilled. Juno is content, her wrath appeased at last. To remove Juturna from the scene the king of the gods sends one of the furies to drive her back to her fountain.

Now the end is near and both champions know it. They taunt each other with angry words, but Turnus says that it is not Aeneas who terrifies him, but the gods, for Jupiter is his enemy. The full realization of the truth of these words seems almost to paralyze him. He picks up a huge stone to heave at Aeneas but the throw is wild and comes nowhere near the hero. Loosing his senses he runs back and forth looking for a way to escape while Aeneas, choosing the right moment, hurls his spear like a shot from a catapult. Its head sinks deep into Turnus' thigh, and he falls to the ground.

A mighty groan up from the lips of the Rutilians, so loud that the whole hillside resounds with the echo. Not a sound comes from the Trojans. Turnus' last words are not a prayer for mercy, but rather an admission of his guilt: "I have deserved this. You have conquered; Lavinia is your wife." With these words he repeats the terms of the treaty. Half-heartedly he pleas for his life which Aeneas is ready to spare until he catches sight of the sword belt of Pallas which Turnus has worn ever since he killed the young man. Revenge and grief well up in his heart. Deep into the breast of his foe Aeneas plunges his sword and "with a groan, life fled to the underworld."

> **COMMENT:** So the end comes to Turnus whose only crime was passion for honor. Yet he was guilty because it was this passion that caused him to start the war, and this passion that made him refuse to stop it. Almost to the last minute he is torn between the false hopes represented by Juno, Juturna, and Faunus, and his heart's desire, to save Italy for her native people, which he cannot abandon. But in the end he turns heroically to death to save his honor and performs a bitter penance by admitting his guilt to Aeneas. The book ends with Aeneas longing to spare Turnus, which is symbolic of Rome's great mission as expressed by Anchises in book VI. But Turnus must die in order that peace, Rome's greatest gift to the world, may come.

NAMES AND PLACES

CYDONIA: important city in Crete, rival of Knossos. Crete was famous for its archers.

SUMMARY: Book XII has three purposes: a.) to complete the picture of Turnus' character; b.) to give a final understanding of Aeneas; and c.) to emphasize the glory of Rome.

a.   The reader is able to visualize Turnus because of the many similes.

> 1.   In the beginning he is compared to a lion slightly wounded, ready to attack the hunters.   But he has lost some of the confidence which he possessed when we met him in Book IX.

> 2.   Then he is compared to a bellowing bull, charging a tree trunk. His efforts are futile because, though his nature is noble, his fighting passion has robbed him of sanity. This passion is symbolized by the appearance of the Fury at the beginning (Allecto, Book VII) and end (Megaera, Book XII) of his career.

> 3.   In the next simile he is not a beast, but Mars, the very god of war himself, driving his wild swift horses. Gradually, however, his strength decreases, foreshadowing the coming catastrophe. His words to Juturna indicate that he expects to die, but with honor. When he first comes on the scene in Book VII, he is sure of divine protection, for Juno is on his side. In the end he says his destruction is due to the hatred of the gods.

> 4.   Then he is compared to a plunging landslide, which hints at defeat.

> 5.   In the final simile, he is a stag in terror of the hunting dogs and nets which are hemming him in. The important thing about his last words is not that he asks for his life, but that he admits his guilt.   Virgil arouses the reader's compassion: as the fourth book ends with the tragedy of Dido, trapped by fatal passion and the interference of the gods (remember that Juno is the deity who represents passion throughout the Aeneid), so in the same way is Turnus trapped by his passion for honor and by the goddesses who prevent his achieving it; and his tragedy is nearly as great.

b.   Aeneas in this book has become almost pure symbol, rather than a flesh and blood hero. Even in his similes, such as the one in which he is compared to a threatening storm, we do not see Aeneas the man so much as the psychological effects of his presence, and, above all, his personification of the Roman concepts of justice and order.

> 1.   In his speech establishing the treaty he promises to "spare the conquered," but when the truce is broken, he must destroy his enemy to fulfill the mission of "crushing the proud."

> 2.   For the sake of justice he is made a martyr, wounded by the unknown arrow, when he attempts to re-establish law and order. It is in this instance that he represents the Roman ideal of waging war only in self-defense. He no longer glories in fighting. It has become a bitter necessity, forced upon him by his obligation to avenge Pallas, which is for Aeneas a duty.

3. He personifies order and civilization, too, when he and his disciplined troops attack Latinus' disorganized city.

4. At the end his tragic memory of Troy is gone forever. His personality has become so bound up with Rome's mission that he is the mythological symbol of her glory.

c. The triumph of Rome is seen in Aeneas defeating Turnus. For Aeneas represents the high ideal of Rome's laws and ethics, while Turnus stands for the natural strength of primitive Italy. The terms of the treaty with Latinus—that both nations would live together as equals—and the last wish of Juno—that the Roman race become powerful because of Italian virtue—symbolically express what Virgil believed: that the joining of these two forces, high ideals and primitive strength, in equal measure, is what produced the political and historical greatness of Rome.

THE ECLOGUES

INTRODUCTION The Eclogues (or as they are more properly called, the Bucolics, from the Greek word meaning rustic) are probably the strangest of all Virgil's works to modern readers. At first glance they seem to be about imaginary shepherds, singing songs which don't make very much sense. They live in a land where everything is lovely. Indeed, the poems are so unrealistic, and so unlike anything in our modern world, that it is hard for us to get in the right mood to appreciate their delicate and wistful beauty. Who cares about ideal shepherds (who seem a bit effeminate) with strange unpronounceable Greek names, anyway? We are forgetting, however, two important factors in such a judgment. First we must remember the period of history in which Virgil wrote. Then we must remember the ancient attitude toward composing poetry, or writing in general.

As has already been mentioned, Virgil's youth was spent in the chaotic years of civil war. Julius Caesar had been the great popular hero. Then he was assassinated. His heirs, Octavius (later to become Augustus) and Marc Antony, defeated the forces of Brutus and Cassius (who by killing Caesar had thought they could salvage the old Republic) at the battle of Philippi in 42 B.C. This temporarily brought an end to the civil war and the fighting, but it left large numbers of veterans clamoring for their pay. The easiest way for the men in power to pay the soldiers was to give them land, and that around Cremona and Mantua in northern Italy was very desirable. But most of it was already owned and under cultivation. This did not matter: farms were taken from men whose families had owned or worked them for generations, and were then handed to the soldiers. The sight of these swaggering intruders on the roads, or in the market place in Mantua, must have been galling indeed. It was only through rare good luck that Virgil himself was not dispossessed. He had met the governor of the territory, Pollio. And fortunately, Pollio was more than a statesman. He was also a man of letters who wrote poetry and who appreciated Virgil's talent. This great man become the young poet's first patron. (Virgil was about twenty-eight at the time.) Possibly he gave Virgil a letter of introduction to Octavius. We do not know exactly what happened because Virgil was extremely reticent. In his poetry he only hinted at his own personal experiences. But from the allusions in the first and ninth Eclogues we can fairly safely assume that Octavius had a hand in enabling Virgil to keep his father's farm. The fact that the poet came so close to loosing his land probably made it doubly dear to him. He loved the country with deep feeling, and the near loss of his farm, which made the frightening results of war so real, were reason enough to pick a pastoral setting for his first mature attempt at poetry.

This brings us to the second thing we must be aware of in reading Virgil, or any other ancient writer. The Greek or Roman author always wrote with a deep sense of the centuries of tradition behind him. Unlike many modern writers and poets, who are determined to rebel and be as different as possible, (though they may not have read enough or studied enough to know what they are rebelling against) the ancient writer was thoroughly steeped in the various forms of literature. The category, poetry, for an example, was classified into epic, elegiac, lyric, pastoral and didactic. A poet-to-be would read and thoroughly digest the best of the previous writers in his field. His one goal was to be as much like the earlier poet as possible, only better.

So Virgil, loving the country, loved the greatest of the Greek pastoral poets, Theocritus. He was a native of Sicily, but did most of his writing in the city which was the great cultural center of the ancient world from 300 to 100 B.C., Alexandria, in Egypt. We do not know the dates of Theocritus' birth or death, but from references in his poems, we can safely say that he wrote "around 275 B.C." Virgil's Eclogues are certainly reminiscent of the Idylls of Theocritus. The majority of the names of his shepherds are Theocritan. Many of the subjects in the Eclogues can be found in the Idylls, for example: the deserted girl inventing a spell to get her lover to come back to her, the nymphs and satyrs mourning the death of a shepherd, or the singing contests. But we need not think that Virgil sat down with a copy of Theocritus' Idylls open in front of him saying, "Hm, I like that line. I will translate it and put it here," or "Theocritus has the shepherd Lycidas, saying these words. I will put them in the mouth of Menalcas, to be a little different." Rather, the Roman poet completely absorbed the Greek poet into the recesses of his mind. Theocritus' vocabulary and settings were the framework within which Virgil created his own pictures. The subjects of these were varied: the beauty of the Italian countryside, the need for friends, his admiration for great statesmen, his sensitivity, to the wrongs done to his neighbors. Perhaps most important of all, into the idyllic frame he placed his burning ideal, the Golden Age of peace.

By careful analysis of the veiled allusions to contemporary men and events, scholars have arrived at dates for the composition of the Eclogues. The outside limits are 43 to 37 B.C. There are ten poems in all. They are brief: the shortest is sixty-three lines, the longest one hundred and eleven lines. In most of them two shepherds either talk or sing together. Sometimes their topics refer to contemporary events, sometimes they are wholly imaginary. The poems were probably not written in the order in which they now are, but were arranged after all ten were finished. In their final order, these poems of light and shadow, joy and sorrow, form an enchanting book, but in order to appreciate it, we must want to put ourselves under its spell. We have been taught to glorify reality, and to scorn the vision and the ideal. But if we truly want to enjoy the Eclogues, we must surrender our passion for realism. There is no "Arcadia" where the climate is always spring, where shepherds sing, and play music all day long. But if we are looking for beauty, pleasure, sensitivity, and the innermost longings of men's hearts, these we will find in the Eclogues.

ECLOGUE I

This poem is the first in the book, but it was probably the last to be written, since it was dedicated to Octavius. By the time Virgil had completed the Eclogues, Octavius had become the most important man of Julius Caesar's heirs. The poet was in his debt because, as has already been mentioned, Octavius was instrumental in enabling Virgil to keep his farm. But all of Virgil's friends were not so fortunate and the poet was both grateful for his own good fortune and sensitive to the sorrows of others. So the subject of the first Eclogue deals with the theme of joy and sadness over having or loosing the land.

Two shepherds, Meliboeus and Tityrus, meet each other one day. It is hot, but the beech tree provides welcome shade. Tityrus is happily playing a love song to Amaryllis on his shepherd's pipe, but Meliboeus is miserable. His lands have been taken from him, and he must go elsewhere. He wonders how Tityrus can be so happy. The latter answers that it is a god who has brought him such joy, or at least he will honor him as a god with a sacrifice of a lamb. Meliboeus is not jealous, for he has a kind heart, but he is curious to know who this god is who has been so good to his friend. Tityrus doesn't answer that right away. First he must tell about his trip to the great city, Rome. He has never been outside his own little town before, and thought all places would be the same. But heavens no! Rome is like a huge tree, and Mantua but a little scraggly bush. He had gone to Rome to buy his freedom. He had saved up money before to buy it, but always his mistress, Galatea, spent what he had saved. Now she had left him, and so with new savings he at last managed to purchase his freedom. It was at Rome that he saw the young god (probably a reference to Octavius) who assured him that he could keep his lands, for he told him that he could feed his oxen as he had in the past, and rear his bulls.

"Lucky old man," is Meliboeus' reaction. And if we close our eyes and see with the imagination, we can understand why. Around him are the well known brooks and the cooling shade. He will still be able to hear the gentle hum of the bees on a hazy day persuading him to sleep as they sip the willow blossoms. And the pigeons which he has tamed will coo gently, because he, Tityrus, has not gone away. The line about the bees is full of wonderful s sounds which are impossible to get in English. They have a remarkable sleep-inducing effect: saepe levi somnum suadebit inire susurro.

But Tityrus is still remembering the face of his young god, and does not even pay much attention when Meliboeus says how unlucky he is. Tityrus may stay, but he has to go and leave behind his cottage with its roof made of cooling clumps of sod. An upstart soldier, who has no feeling for the sacred beauty of his plot of ground and over which he has struggled so long to get it to produce, has taken his farm. It is foolish of him to think about it any more. He'd best be going. Where he will pasture his goats, he has no idea.

Tityrus wakes out of his reverie long enough to ask Meliboeus to spend the night with him. He has plenty to eat, apples, chestnuts, pressed cheeses; what more could he want? If he looks over in the distance he can see smoke rising from chimneys, showing that evening meals are being readied. The shadows from the mountains stretch longer across the valley.

We will never know whether Meliboeus went with his more fortunate friend that night, or not. But we are left with a tantalizing taste of beauty as the shadows lengthen. It is a hard thing that so much of the beauty rests not only in the descriptions of the countryside, but in the melody of the Latin words themselves. Perhaps more than any other work of Virgil, the Eclogues are poems of pure delight in sound.

ECLOGUE II

This Eclogue is probably the first one Virgil wrote. It has no hidden references as far as we know, but is just a simple story of unrequited love. The poem also shows how thoroughly Virgil had absorbed the beauty of his model, Theocritus. (In Theocritus' third idyll a rejected lover complains, and in the eleventh the Cyclops, Polyphemus, cries out against the cruelty of Galatea.)

Corydon is madly in love with his master's favorite slave, Alexis. The sentiment is not returned. Every day Corydon pours out his misery to the hills and woods. "Cruel Alexis, have you no pity? You will drive me to my death pretty soon." Perhaps it would be more sensible to love temperamental Amaryllis, or Menalcas, even though he is dark. Alexis counts too much on his fair complexion. White flowers, as well as dark ones get picked. How is it possible that Alexis can scorn him, when he is rich, as well as good looking? He has enough cows to have fresh milk all year long. And the other day when the sea was calm—well, it was quite a pleasant reflection!

Oh Alexis, we could be so happy together. The happiness would make your singing more beautiful than the songs of Pan, the god of shepherd's music himself. I will give you a shepherd's pipe, and two young spotted roes. I've been saving them for you, but since you are so disdainful, I may give them to Thestylis instead. She likes all my gifts.

All nature is beautiful in your honor, Alexis. The woodland nymphs will bring baskets piled high with white lilies, pale blue violets, and bright red poppies. Others offer lovely sweet-smelling herbs, hyacinths and marigolds. I, Corydon, will pick quinces, chestnuts and plums, and present them in a bed of fragrant laurel and myrtle. Foolish Corydon! Such gifts can not possibly touch proud Alexis. I am indulging in wild day-dreams, chasing after Alexis as a lion stalks a wolf, a wolf a goat, or as a playful goat pursues the flowering clover. All day long, till the shadows lengthen, the madness of love seizes Corydon. I have done nothing worthwhile the whole time. Look how my vines need pruning. There is always another Alexis.

Or is there? The reader wonders. The theme of the little poem is simple enough. But the story of the rejected lover has its setting in a riotous array of fragrances and colors. Perhaps a deeper theme is the sheer enjoyment of beauty.

ECLOGUE III

In this eclogue we find a definite historical reference: It is the name,
Pollio. Gaius Asinius Pollio was an important man who attached himself
in his youth to Julius Caesar, and then to Antony after Caesar's assassination.
Octavius had high respect for his literary judgment, but he never really
won Pollio over to his side after Antony was defeated in 31 B.C. He was
one of the first of a series of men to aid Virgil by encouragement and
financial support so that he could write poetry. And in this poem Virgil
voices his gratitude. The eclogue is different from the first two, in that
it is not just conversation between two shepherds. The central section
is a singing contest, much in the nature of a parlor game. One shepherd
sings a line, and the second must either develop that line or think of a
comparable subject, or one opposite to it. Virgil possibly got his idea
for this from two idylls of Theocritus, XIV and XV. This type of contest
has a lovely Greek name: amoebaean, which means responsive singing.
In this poem the contestants are Menalcas and Damoetas. Palaemon is
the judge.

In the beginning the two are quarreling with each other, half in earnest,
half in jest. Menalcas teases Damoetas for not being a very reliable
shepherd. The other retorts that he should know what he is talking about,
when he spends his time flirting and making love in the little wooded chapel
over there. Or there was another day when he broke the bow and arrow
someone had given to Daphnis, out of pure spite. Now it is Menalcas'
turn to think up accusations, for he caught Damoetas trying to catch a
goat that belonged to Damon. But Damoetas has an answer for that too.
The goat was his by right, since he had beaten Damon in singing. At that
Menalcas pretends a great laugh of incredulity. Damoetas beat someone
in singing? Why he couldn't even carry a tune! Damoetas retaliates by
daring him to try a match right now. He will wager a cow, a really good
milker. Menalcas is willing enough but refuses to bet an animal since
that would get him in trouble with his father and nasty step-mother. But
he has two beautifully carved wooden cups. They show two famous astronomers,
and the best seasons for harvest and ploughing; and they are brand new.
To Damoetas, that is hardly a fair exchange, so he brings out his two
cups, made by the same carver as Menalcas'. Then Menalcas replies that
he can not get off that easily. He will find something to equal the heifer.
And they drag a passing shepherd over to be the judge. "Go ahead, sing,
since we are seated on the soft grass. Now every field, every tree is
putting out shoots; the woods are in leaf, and it is truly the most beautiful
time of year."

Damoetas begins with two lines about Jupiter, who is the beginning of all
living things. Menalcas responds by singing of Phoebus Apollo, to whom
he gives laurel and budding hyacinths. (The Latin word used to describe
the hyacinth means growing red, or darker, in color, which is what happens
as the hyacinth buds open.) Next come two answering couplets about the
ones they love. Galatea throws apples at Damoetas to catch his attention,
and then runs coyly off. Menalcas' flame, Amyntas, comes to him of his
own accord. His dogs know the boy as well as they do the moon, Delia.
Next they sing of the gifts for the beloved, a pair of turtle doves, and ten
perfect ripe apples. Following this are two couplets telling how happily
they spend the hours together. Perhaps it would be better to say "spent"
the hours together, for now Damoetas turns to a new love, Phyllis. Menalcas

pretends to take the part of another shepherd, Iollas, who loves Phyllis to distraction. Then Damoetas abruptly changes the subject to sing of unhappy things: the wolf is cruel to the flock, a sudden downpour to the crops, a high wind to the trees, but above all is the anger of Amaryllis to him. Menalcas picks the opposite thought. A shower is kind to the corn, the shade of the willow to the flock, and Amyntas to him.

Amyntas' kindness makes Damoetas remember Pollio, who had kind words for his simple poetry. Menalcas reminds him that Pollio is a poet too. Damoetas becomes almost ecstatic about how wonderful Pollio is, so Menalcas changes the subject to talk about bad poets. To like such awful poets as Bavius and Maevius is worse than trying to milk he-goats and harness foxes. This brings Damoetas back to the more everyday subjects, of flocks, bulls, and the dangers of snakes. The contest ends with each singer proposing an unanswerable riddle to the other. The judge cannot possibly give the prize to either shepherd. Each one has been perfect. "It is time now to close off the canals, boys; the fields have drunk enough."

The poem comes abruptly to an end. It is as if we had been looking at an impressionistic painting for a while, and then the guards in the museum turned the lights off. We may not even be exactly sure what the picture was about, but we do remember it was lovely. And as ever, with Virgil, the sounds of the syllables flowing into one another have a magic that cannot be quite so perfect in English.

ECLOGUE IV

With the fourth eclogue we leave behind the everyday subjects of shepherds and see a different side of Virgil's soul, the deeply religious side, in love with the hope for a Golden Age. It has been called the "Messianic Eclogue" because its theme is the birth of a child who will bring the age of peace with him. Volumes of words have been written to explain who the child is, but the most logical idea is to guess that the birth of a son to Pollio, Virgil's acknowledged patron by now, gave the poet the idea. Whatever the answer, the indentity of the child has little bearing on the understanding of the poem. In it we find Virgil, the visionary, describing the not-quite-impossible dream which has beguiled man through the ages: there shall come a time of peace.

"Muses of Sicily (the home of Theocritus), let me take a somewhat nobler subject for my poetry." So Virgil tells us he is going to go beyond the topics of his model, Theocritus. This poem must be worthy of a consul, (Pollio was one of the consuls of the year 40 B.C.) The last age, prophesied by the Cumaean Sibyl is now come. (See names and places at the end of the Eclogue.) The virgin Justice, who was last of the immortals to leave the earth at the end of Saturn's Golden Age, will come back again. A boy is being born; Diana be kind to him, for with him comes the new generation bringing the second Golden Age. And Pollio shall be covered with glory because it is in his consulship that the longed-for age begins. Gods and heroes will again walk the earth with men and the child shall rule all with peace.

While he is young the whole world of nature will bring him gifts. No one will have to cultivate the soil, for the bounties of the earth will grow and produce of their own accord. Goats will come home by themselves to be milked. Lions will not hurt the sheep, and snakes will disappear. But when the child is older he will learn of the deeds of his father and of the heroes of old. And that is necessary, for not all men will take to peaceful ways immediately. There will probably be another Trojan war. By the time the child is grown, however, men will no longer need to trade, for each land will produce all that it uses. The earth will know no plough nor the oxen the yoke. Men will not have to dye wool for the colors will grow naturally on the sheep themselves.

"Run on, ages like these," said the Fates talking about the divine power of destiny to their spindles. Here Virgil perhaps suggests that the Fates are singing a birthday song to the tiny boy. The child must truly be descended from the gods, from Jupiter himself, for the vault of heaven bows to him. If only he, Virgil, can live long enough to tell of the child's wonderful deeds! He must be the equal of Orpheus, or Apollo, or even Pan with the whole of Arcadia to judge him. As for the tiny boy, soon he shall smile up at his mother. This is a good omen, pointing toward a glorious career. Until he smiles at his parents, no child can receive the favors of the gods.

What a strange poem! But we must remember that it was written in a time when the stable order of the old days of the Republic had come crashing down around men's ears. Nothing was certain. One day you had land, the next it belonged to a soldier. One day Julius Caesar was the most important man in the government; the next day he no longer existed. Today Antony is loved by the faction in power; tomorrow, beware of Octavius.

Pollio is consul and he has been good to Virgil. So Virgil praises him but he avoids going to disgusting extremes as men often did in praising their benefactors. He starts quietly, not even mentioning Pollio's name at first, but only saying that the poem will be worthy of a consul. Further on he mentions the consul's name. Then he says "under your leadership" which almost amounts to calling him the savior of the state. Rome will atone for her terrible guilt of ceaseless warfare while he is their leader.

So Virgil gives vent to his intensely mystical feelings, and in the Middle Ages he was thought of as a Christian who had lived too early, and yet had prophesied the coming of Christ. But what poet of sensitivity would not dream of a golden age, if he had lived all his life in the insecurity of constant civil war? Thus Virgil hopes, and we are lucky indeed to have his golden words.

NAMES AND PLACES

CUMAEAN SIBYL: uttered prophecies which were written on leaves and recorded in the Sibylline books. The Sibyl lived near modern Naples. One of her prophecies said that there was a succession of ages, gold, silver, etc., the last of which was the age of the sun god, Apollo. The other prophecy had the idea of a Great Year which covered considerable length of time. At the end of this Great Year, the stars and planets would be back in the same position in which they had started. This Great Year was divided into ten cycles and Virgil imagines that the last cycle of one Great Year is over, and a new one will begin with the second Golden Age.

SATURN: a mythical king in Italy who ruled during the Golden Age.

LUCINA: the name used for the goddess Diana when she was presiding over childbirth.

APOLLO: the sun god, and the god of healing. He was also the god of punishment, the god of song and music, and the god of prophecy. He was the twin brother of Diana.

TIPHYS: the helmsman of the Argo.

ARGO: the ship which the mythical hero, Jason, built to go and get the Golden Fleece from Colchis, at the eastern end of the Black Sea.

ACHILLES: the greatest of the Greek heroes in the war against Troy.

FATES: three goddesses who were sisters. Clotho spins the thread of life, Lachesis draws it out, and Atropos cuts it.

ORPHEUS: famous poet-musician of legends, went down to the under-world to get his wife Eurydice back. He played so beautifully for the queen of the underworld, Proserpina, that his wish was granted, on the condition that he not look around at her till he reached earth. At the last minute he turns around to be sure that Eurydice is still following; he looses her forever.

LINUS: thought to be the first composer of dirges, and according to some traditions a son of Apollo.

CALLIOPE: the muse of epic poetry. The nine muses were the inspiring goddesses of poetry, song and dance, and of the arts and sciences.

PAN: the great god of flocks and shepherds. He was considered the inventor of the shepherd's pipe. Originally he was the special god of Arcadia, a part of south central Greece.

ECLOGUE V

Now we come to traditional themes for this eclogue. It is another singing contest and, as in the third eclogue, there is a reference to a historical person. This time it is more veiled, but still it is fairly certain that the Daphnis in the poem is Julius Caesar, whom Virgil, as well as many others regarded as a national hero. He was deified, that is, proclaimed a god, in 42 B.C. by a vote of the senate and people. Virgil alludes to this in the poem. In fact he is rather consistently a hero worshiper, whether it be Pollio, Julius Caesar, or eventually, Augustus.

Mopsus and Menalcas meet and decide to sing verses and play the pipe. Mopsus is skilled on the musical instrument, Menalcas at composing poetry. The question is whether to sit under the shade of a tree where the breeze will cool them, or whether to rest at the entrance to the cave where the wild vine is climbing. They decide for the latter; and Menalcas asks Mopsus to start, since the only shepherd who claims to play any better than he is Amyntas. Mopsus says he will sing a song he composed recently, rather than play his shepherd's pipe. Talking back and forth this way they arrive at the cave. When they are settled comfortably, Mopsus begins.

His song tells the story of how a beautiful shepherd, Daphnis, died before his time. The nymphs wept, and his mother cried out at the cruelty of fate. No cattle grazed in the fields or drank in the streams. Even lions in Africa groaned aloud at his death. There never was a shepherd like Daphnis. He led the dances of Bacchus, harnessing tigers to his chariot. On his tomb it says that he was known as far as the stars.

Menalcas interrupts to praise Mopsus for his singing, saying that it is more delightful than sleep is to the weary, or clear running water to the thirsty. But it is his turn to praise Daphnis to the skies. He imagines Daphnis on the threshold of Olympus looking at the stars and the clouds beneath his feet. All of nature, the shepherds, and their beloved Pan, rejoice as Daphnis becomes a god. No more does the wolf stalk the sheep or men hem in the stag with their hunting nets. Daphnis loves repose. The very mountains and virgin forests fling their joyous voices to the stars; even the rocks and bushes resound: "A god, he is a god, Menalcas."

Then the song changes from one of praise to one of petition. Now that Daphnis is a god, Menalcas begs him to be kind to those who love him. They will worship him at the same time they worship Apollo, and pour out fresh foaming milk in his honor. Olive oil and wine will be their offerings twice a year, with a gay festival of singing and dancing pantomimes. They will perform these rites as long as the bees feed on sweet-smelling thyme, or grasshoppers sip the dew.

In turn for such a beautiful song, Mopsus wants to give something to his friend. The melody is more lovely than the south wind as it comes up, or the sound of the surf on the shore; more beautiful than water as it tumbles down a rocky stream-bed. So the two shepherds exchange gifts. Menalcas gives the pipe on which he has played "Corydon is on fire for beautiful Alexis," and "Whose sheep are those? Meliboeus'?" (These are portions of the opening lines of the second and third eclogues.) Mopsus gives his carefully carved shepherd's crook. The little scene is over.

The poem is unusual because it contains both a lament and a consolation. Generally a poem was devoted entirely to either one or the other of these subjects. It is impossible to prove that Virgil, in exalting Daphnis, is praising Caesar. The mention of Bacchus may refer to Caesar's reemphasis of the god's worship. Virgil may have introduced Apollo, because Caesar's birthday fell during the festival of Apollo. Whatever the inner purpose of this poem may be, the sounds of lamenting and rejoicing nature are beautiful in themselves.

ECLOGUE VI

This poem is perhaps a panegyric (writing in praise of a person or an event) for Alfenus Varus, the governor of Cisalpine Gaul. Varus had asked Virgil to write some lines commemorating his valor in the civil wars. The poet hints that he would like to write epic, but he doesn't feel mature enough yet. So he tries his hand at scientific philosophy, in the manner of his great idol, Lucretius. (Lucretius had written a long poem explaining the origin of the universe. There was no vindictive god as the creator, only atoms and void. The infinite variety of the combinations of atoms and void accounted for all the forms of animate and inanimate existence.)

So the eclogue starts out with an apology for not writing epic in honor of Varus. Then the poet summons the muses (Pierian maids) to help him. The scene opens with the satyr Silenus, drunk again, or rather passed out completely, in his cave. He is still clutching the handle of his wine bowl when two shepherds, Chromis and Mnasyllus, find him. The garlands that he had draped around his head are scattered all over the place. With these the playful boys tie Silenus up, and then paint his red face even redder with the juice from mulberries. The satyr comes to, and laughs, promising to sing. But the song he sings is wondrously strange, so much so that even the oak tree nods its upper branches.

The song concerns the miraculous transformations in nature. Atoms of earth, air, water and fire hurtle together through space to form the globe of the world. Little by little the land solidifies and separates from the ocean. Soon life develops, thanks to the sun and showers. Trees grow up and living creatures roam the unknown mountains. So far Virgil is following Lucretius, but now, to explain the wondrous miracle of man, he turns to myth.

After the flood, Pyrrha threw stones behind her, which sprang up into men; she had been told to do this with the bones of her mother, in order to repeople the world. She finally decided that the earth was her mother, and that stones must be her mother's bones. Then came the Golden Age of Saturn, and Prometheus, whose thefts put an end to it. (See Names and Places for detail.) The sad tale of Hylas, stolen from Hercules by the water-nymphs, and Pasiphaë, in love with a snow white bull, are the next subjects in Silenus' song.

Then suddenly he shifts from myth to contemporary times, and sings of Gallus (a poet and dear friend of Virgil) wandering by the river of Permessus, sacred to the Muses. One of these gives Gallus the pipes which had been given to the ancient Greek poet, Hesiod (born in Ascra in Boeotia). With these pipes he will then be able to sing of the favorite groves of Apollo.

Finally the satyr goes back to his mythology, ending with the story of the changing of Scylla into a monster, and princess Philomela into a nightingale. All these themes make up the multi-colored patchwork of Silenus' song, and the pulsating valleys reecho the sound to the stars "until the shadows of evening, ordering the flocks to be led to their stables and be counted one by one, advanced over Olympus, which was not yet ready for night."

This poem is full of the joy in nature and song which is such an important aspect of Virgil's temperament. But it also shows his knowledge for philosophy, and his yearning for fundamental truths of the universe which made him so dear to the Christians of the Middle Ages. The satyr's song has three parts, setting forth the three parts of Virgil's creed: (their fullest exposition is in the <u>Aeneid</u>:) science, myth (symbolizing the inexplicable and thus miraculous aspects of the universe), and history. All these are interrelated, for science (the study of first beginnings), preceeds myth (the study of pre—history), which comes before known events and people. Thus we find Virgil, in a seemingly light—hearted mood, pondering most seriously the ultimate questions of life.

NAMES AND PLACES

<u>CYNTHIUS</u>: a name for Apollo, derived from Mt. Cynthus on the island of Delos, the god's birthplace.

<u>FAUNS</u>: the followers of the woodland god, Faunus. Faunus is mentioned quite interchangeably with Pan, as the Fauns are with Satyrs. These last were a class of beings associated with the worship of Bacchus. They represented the luxuriously virile side of nature, and so were thought of as indulging in every sensual pleasure. They were usually portrayed as having horns and goats feet, round, turned—up noses, and a horse's tail.

<u>RHODOPE</u>: one of the highest mountain ranges in Thrace, sacred to Bacchus, the god of wine; also, the country of the Orpheus legend.

<u>PARNASSUS</u>: the highest part of the mountain range north of Delphi in Greece. It was thought to be the favorite haunt of Apollo and the muses, and thus a source of inspiration for poetry and song.

<u>ISMARUS</u>: a mountain in Thrace noted for its vineyards.

<u>NEREUS</u>: a lesser sea divinity, father of fifty maidens, or sea—nymphs, called Nereids.

<u>PYRRHA</u>: and her husband Deucalion were the only mortals left on earth after Jupiter sent the great flood. (The Greek myth has a certain similarity to the story of Noah and the Ark.)

<u>PROMETHEUS</u>: stole fire from the gods to give it to men when Jupiter withheld it. He also taught men about architecture, medicine, mathematics, and writing, all contrary to the will of Jupiter. He was chained to various mountains, among which were the Caucasus, where his liver was slowly devoured by an eagle.

<u>HYLAS</u>: was loved by the great super-hero, Hercules. When he went to draw water from a fountain he was pulled into the water by the nymphs (Naiads) because of his beauty. Hercules searched for him all over, calling out his name. The only answer he got was what sounded like an echo from the depths of a spring.

<u>PASIPHAË</u>: wife of the king of Crete, Minos. She had the misfortune to fall in love with the sacred bull. (It wasn't completely her fault as the god of the sea, Neptune, inspired her with this passion to get even with Minos.) She thus became the mother of the Minotaur.

<u>DICTE</u>: a mountain in Crete.

<u>HESPERIDES</u>: Nymphs who guarded the golden apples which earth gave to Juno (the queen of the gods) at her marriage to Jupiter (the king of of the gods). It was one of these apples which Atalanta stooped down to admire when it was thrown at her feet. She was racing against a suitor, Hippomenes, (Milanion, according to some) who threw the apple to delay her. He thus won the race, and her hand in marriage.

PHAËTHON: one of Apollo's sons who insisted on driving the sun-god's chariot.   He was too young to control the horses and almost set the earth on fire by driving so low.   So Jupiter killed him with a thunderbolt. His sisters were changed into poplar trees.

PERMESSUS: a river in Boeotia whose source is on Mt. Helicon.

AONIA: the section of Boeotia where Mt. Helicon was located.

GRYNEA: a town in Asia Minor where there was a temple and oracle of Apollo.   Virgil is paying Gallus the highest tribute when he says that what Gallus has written is worthy of Hesiod, one of the earliest Greek poets.   His writings glorified work.   Although there are many other eulogies of Gallus because of his beautiful poetry, only part of one line of it has come down to us.

SCYLLA: the daughter of Nisus.   She fell in love with Minos, king of Crete, and helped him to conquer her father's city, Megara.   Minos thought this so unnatural that he eventually drowned her.   There is another Scylla, the daughter of a sea god.   She had six heads which seized sailors off ships when they came to close to her rock which was on the Italian side of the straits between Italy and Sicily.   Her lower half was surrounded with barking dogs.   Virgil jumbles the two stories, probably on purpose.

TEREUS: mythical king in Thrace, married one of two sisters whose name was Procne.   Later he hid Procne so he could marry her sister, Philomela.   When Procne learned what had happened she served up their son for supper to Tereus and then fled with her sister.   When Tereus was just about to catch them they were changed into birds, a swallow and a nightingale.

EUROTAS: one of the largest rivers in southern Greece, flowing by Sparta.

ECLOGUE VII

There seems to be no clue to the time when Virgil wrote this eclogue for it has no references to contemporary people or events. It is one of his poems of almost pure fantasy, another contest in singing, full of echoes from Theocritus.

The contest has already taken place, and Meliboeus is telling about it. Daphnis had summoned him to listen to the singing of two shepherds, Corydon and Thyrsis. So they went down to the banks of the Mincio (the river flowing by Mantua, Virgil's birthplace), leaving their goats to tend themselves. Corydon began, says Meliboeus, with a prayer to the Muses, that his song would be as good as the one Codrus sang, for Codrus rivaled Apollo. Thyrsis' reply is that he hopes Codrus sides will burst with envy at his beautiful song. Still, he doesn't want to provoke the jealousy of the gods by too much self-praise, so he will put a sprig of foxglove on his forehead to ward off any evil tongue. (We see in the two shepherds the contrast between the modest and boastful singer.)

The next theme is what the shepherds will offer to the gods. Corydon, pretending to be the young shepherd, Micon, will offer Diana a boar's head, and a pair of antlers; if she continues to be kind to him, he will erect a marble statue of the goddess. Thyrsis says that he will give the garden scarecrow god, Priapus, a bowl of milk and some flat cornmeal cakes. These are all his poor garden can produce at the moment. He is a marble statue now, but if things pick up, he will be replaced by a golden one. (Here we see the contrast between the sensible and the absurd, for who ever heard of a scarecrow made out of marble, much less made out of gold!)

Corydon then asks his love, Galatea, who is sweeter than thyme and whiter than swans, to meet him in the early evening when the herd returns to the barns. And Thyrsis misses the point altogether, and hears only the mention of the word "thyme," and the reference to sundown: "May I seem more bitter than Sardinian herbs, if this day isn't longer than a whole year," is his rejoinder. Annoyed with not being very bright at the game of matching or properly contrasting a subject, he wants to go home. But Corydon is enjoying the game, and sings of the cool delights that protect men and beasts from the summer heat: moss-covered springs, grass softer than sleep, the wild strawberry tree offering shade that is hard to find. In reply, Thyrsis takes the opposite season, winter, and the hearth fire that provides the needed warmth. But he says that shepherds do not care about the cold weather, if they have such a fire, any more than wolves do about the number of the sheep, or rushing floods care about their banks. His comparisons are not very suitable, for shepherds who guard flocks should not be compared to destructive forces like floods and wolves. Poor Thyrsis! He tries hard, but he is not having very much success.

In the next pair of themes, however, Thyrsis manages a little better. Corydon sings of nature lamenting when the loved one departs, so Thyrsis sings of the joy in nature when his beloved, Phyllis, returns. The parched field, the thirsty grass, all will turn green and flourishing, and Jupiter will come down in a happy shower. (The only thing that is slightly wrong is that Phyllis may get wet!)

The final theme Corydon picks is that of his favorite trees: the poplar belongs to Hercules, the grape vine to Bacchus, the myrtle to Venus, and the laurel to Apollo. But since Phyllis likes hazels best, they are his favorite tree too. Thyrsis answers by telling where the different kinds of trees grow. He finishes by saying that his dear Lycidas is better than any tree. Of course Lycidas is better than a tree, but Corydon's contrast was not between people and trees, but between which tree was loveliest. So Meliboeus finishes his story of the singing contest by saying that, naturally, Corydon won.

This poem is sort of a companion to the third eclogue where the two singers were so well matched that it was a toss-up. Its subtle theme is an exercise in good taste. Thyrsis shows himself boastful, absurd, temperamental, and often missing the point altogether. And through the lines the sun and the shadows flicker, the brooks gurgle, and music fills the air.

ECLOGUE VIII

Here we again find Virgil alluding to contemporary events. The poem is dedicated to some patron who is sailing up the Illyrian coast. This can be no one else but Pollio, who returned from his campaign in Dalmatia in 39 B.C. The unnamed patron is also a great writer of tragedy, and we know from many other references in ancient authors, that Pollio (unfortunately, none of his works survive) was an excellent writer of poetry and tragedy. The poem is different from the other eclogues in that it has a running refrain which builds up a pitch of magical incantation at the end. (Virgil develops the theme of magical incantation to its most perfect form in the fourth book of the Aeneid.) The idea of the refrain probably came from the first and second Idyls of Theocritus; the magic spell also occurs in his second Idyl.

Virgil starts out by telling of a contest in singing which was so lovely that it charmed heifers and lynxes, and even rivers stopped flowing. The singers were Damon and Alphesiboeus. So beautiful was the song that perhaps Pollio will be willing to listen to a retelling. Maybe the great man will twine a bit of ivy with his laurel crown, given to him as a sign of having won a great victory on the field of battle.

Damon sings first, leaning sadly on his shepherd's crook. Lucifer, the morning star, may rise in a beautiful sky, but the day will be his last, since false Nysa is marrying Mopsus. If only he could sing the exquisite songs from the region of Mt. Maenalus, in Arcadia, to show what an absurd couple they will be. It is worse than if griffins mated with mares, or dogs with deer. He sees in imagination the wedding festivities, the jokes, and the throwing nuts, and cannot bear the thought. For he remembers so clearly when he first saw Nysa. He was but a boy and went with his mother to help Nysa pick apples. But though he could barely reach the lowest branches, he was old enough to fall in love with her.

What a terrible creature is love! Love drove Medea to murder her own children. Who the more cruel of the two was, love, or Medea, he cannot say. But as far as he is concerned, this marriage might as well bring the end of the world, for the most absurd things will come to pass. Wolves will be afraid of sheep; oaks will produce apples; owls will be as beautiful as swans; and clumsy, unmusical Tityrus will sing as beautifully as the king of musicians himself, glorious Orpheus. For Damon there is no hope; he will plunge into the sea from the top of a mountain crag. Let the Maenalian songs come to an end.

So Alphesiboeus answers with a song of incantation as a love charm. He sings of a girl abandoned by her lover, Daphnis. He has gone to town, looking for the beautiful girls there. She will try magic to set her cold-hearted lover on fire again. With magic songs one can bring down the moon. With magic song Circe cast spells on the followers of Ulysses and changed them into beasts. So the girl takes a wax image of her lover and winds threads around it three times, for the gods take pleasure in uneven numbers. She weaves three colors into three knots, and then melts the little figure in the fire. In such a way Daphnis will melt for her. He will long for her as a heifer does for a bull. Now she burns the trinkets he gave her, and when the fire has gone out, she throws the ashes back over her head. All of a sudden, there is a barking at the cottage door. "cease, oh cease now your magic songs! Daphnis has returned from the city."

Heifers and lynxes have been charmed with the singing, and so have we, for the return of Daphnis is the greatest magic of all.

NAMES AND PLACES

OETA: a range of mountains in southern Thessaly.
TIMAVUS: a small river in the north of Italy flowing into the Adriatic.
TMARUS: a mountain in Epirus.
GARAMANTES: the southernmost group of people living in North Africa that were known to the ancients.
MEDEA: killed her two children when her husband, Jason, deserted her for another woman.
CIRCE: an enchantress whom Ulysses encountered in his fabulous travels. She charmed his followers into beasts, but Ulysses was able to trick her and eventually rescued his men.
PONTUS: a region on the south eastern shore of the Black Sea.

ECLOGUE IX

This poem alludes to the unhappy subject mentioned in the first eclogue, the poor farmer thrown off his lands so that some veteran, completely ignorant of farming, might be paid for his services in the wars. Thus it falls in the class of eclogues which deal with contemporary matters. It also seems to contain veiled references to some of the poets of Virgil's day. The names of the various shepherds perhaps stand for some of the poets who were attempting to write pastoral works. But the clues are too vague to follow.

Moeris and Lycidas start out on the path to the city. This time it is Moeris who has lost his plot of ground, and the goats must go to a new master. Lycidas reminds him that one shepherd, Menalcas, was able to save his farm by the power of his song. (This may be a reference to Virgil whose farm was restored.) Moeris remembers, but says that the music of poetry is hard to hear above the sounds of war. In fact it was only because of the timely warning of a crow that he, Moeris, and Menalcas are still alive. How dreadful that would have been, Lycidas replies, to have lost both the singer and his songs. Who would have put into Latin the lovely verses of Theocritus? Or who would have sung in honor of Varus, our governor? For though he, Lycidas, does compose poetry occasionally, the lines sound more like the cackling of geese than melodious swans.

Moeris remembers some more lines that the great Menalcas had adapted from Theocritus about Galatea and quivering poplar trees, and the mottled shade of tangled vines. Lycidas answers that he heard some lovely songs coming from Moeris himself long ago, about the planets and the comet which appeared shortly after Caesar's death. Oh yes, Moeris remembers when he wrote those words, but now he is getting older, and his memory is not what it once was. If Lycidas wants songs he should go to Menalcas. Some other time perhaps, Lycidas thinks. Now the peaceful time of twilight is coming, not a breath of air stirs, the whole expanse of the sea is still. The two of them sing to make the trip to town more pleasant. The other replies that the music will be better when the master singer himself is present. And they walk on in the dusk.

This poem is not meant to be autobiographical, although many critics want it to be. It shows Virgil's skill in stitching quotations from Theocritus onto his own patchwork quilt. Each little piece, whether it be a direct translation of Theocritus, or a shady scene from Virgil's imagination, is unlike any other. And each is utterly beautiful in itself. The brilliant colors are sewn together and we have a creation which is exquisitely pleasing. And with Virgil the pleasure is not only to the eye, but always also to the ear.

ECLOGUE X

The scene of this final poem is Virgil's imaginary Arcadia. But it is written in honor of a real person, Virgil's friend the poet Gallus. In fact it is possible that some of the lines are taken from Gallus' own poetry, as a sign of high tribute. In the eclogue we see evidence of Virgil's longing for friends coupled with his need for men to look up to. As Pollio was his greatest ideal of a patron and poet, so Gallus was his dearest poet-friend.

The poet sings to the echoing woods the story of Gallus' unrequited love. Where were the nymphs then, and why did they not come to comfort the poet in his grief? Why did they linger on the top of Mt. Parnassus or by the fountain Aganippe, while Gallus was weeping all alone under the shadow of Mt. Maenalus? The rest of nature mourned, at any rate, the laurels and the sheep. The shepherds and the swineherds came, and Menalcas, still wet from gathering acorns for the cattle. Even Apollo came asking about Gallus' love. His dear Lycoris has gone after another man, following him through ice and snow, and into army camp too. Silvanus, the protector of boundaries of shepherd's property, approaches, wearing a crown of lilies twined with fennel. Pan himself the god of Arcadia, joins the group of sorrowing friends, and tells Gallus that it doesn't do any good to cry. Tears will not take away the pain. Rather, Love lives on tears as grass does on the water from brooks, or bees on clover.

Gallus sadly answers that he would love to be a simple shepherd in Arcadia, in love with Phyllis or dark-skinned Amyntas, but it is hopeless. There can be no joy in Arcadia unless Lycoris shares it. The passion of his love will force him to join the army, for Lycoris has gone after a soldier who is stationed in the cold Alps. But no, it is better to try and become a shepherd after all, and carve the story of his love on the trees. He will roam over Mt. Maenalus with the nymphs, and hunt boars. Oh, if only such action could heal his wretched disease! But there is no cure, neither in songs, nor in the beauty of the nymphs, or the quiet of the forests. Even if he dares the greatest deeds imaginable, Love will not leave him in peace. He could brave the snows of Thrace, or the scorching heat of Africa, and the anguish of his love would still be with him. "Love conquers all things; let me then yield to love."

These are the humble verses a shepherd has composed for love of Gallus. While he sat watching his flocks and weaving reed baskets he kept thinking of Gallus, and how dear he was. But now it is time to drive the goats home. The shadows lengthen, and they may be as bad for singers as they are for the corn. Sometimes the shade from the junipers even causes blight. "Go on home, goats, you have grazed long enough. The Evening star is rising."

With these words Virgil says farewell to simple shepherd poetry. He does not make any statements about how great or famous he is going to be. He does not say that he is going to attempt a more elevated subject. Quietly he brings his group of ten poems to an end, as a goatherd, looking up and noticing the bright evening star in the red glow of sunset, quietly gets up, and drives his flock home.

NAMES AND PLACES

ARETHUSA: a fountain in Sicily and home of the nymph Arethusa. She is invoked as the muse who inspired Theocritus.

DORIS: the wife of the sea divinity, Nereus. Here her name is given to the body of water under which Arethusa fled to escape the river god, Alpheus.

PINDUS: the name of the chain of mountains which separates Thessaly and Epirus.

AGANIPPE: a fountain on Mt. Helicon in Boeotia.

LYCAEUS: a mountain in Arcadia, sacred to both Jupiter and Pan in Euboea.

CHALCHIS: in Euboea the native city of Euphorion, a poet who lived and wrote in Alexandria in Egypt (around 220 B.C.) Gallus used him as one of his models for his poetic style.

PARTHENIUS: a mountain in Arcadia.

CYDONIAN: means Cretan, from the name of the city in Crete, Cydonia.

HEBRUS: one of the few ice-bound rivers that the Romans knew about. It is the principal river in Thrace.

THE GEORGICS

INTRODUCTION.   To fully understand the Georgics of Virgil, we need to know something of the two earlier poets whose writings greatly influenced the composition of the book.   The first of these was the eighth century Greek poet, Hesiod, a native of Ascra in Boeotia.   His poem, the Works and Days, was addressed to his brother, Perses.   Perses had wronged Hesiod by trying to bribe judges to take away Hesiod's share of the inheritance left them by their father.   So the poem is written with the idea of showing Perses how wrong he is.   The basic themes of the work are Justice, Contentment, Hard Work, and Religion.   Hesiod writes about farming and the seasons only to illustrate the value of hard work.   He also discusses a number of religious and social taboos.   The whole poem, however, is aimed at showing his brother that he ought to be good.

Virgil's poem, though it has many similarities, is written with a much more universal aim.   It contains three of Hesiod's ideas, contentment, hard work, and religion.   But it has one transcending theme, the theme of peace: peace for Virgil's beloved Italy, and peace for men's souls.   It is in connection with this second type of peace that we must turn to Virgil's other great model, Lucretius.

Lucretius was a Roman poet, about a generation older than Virgil.   His poem of six books, On the Nature of Things, is a scientific-philosophic treatise.   Its main purpose was to free men from superstitious fears so that they could have peace of mind.   According to Lucretius' doctrine, there is nothing in nature which does not have a scientific explanation, and the gods are not concerned with the affairs of men.   Everything in the universe is composed of the same two substances, atoms and void.   But since there are an infinite number of atoms, there are infinite varieties of combinations.   This explains the diversity in nature.   Yet there is much more than just science in his book.   It is filled with many majestic passages of poetry which inspired Virgil as much as the philosophy of peace of mind.   For this reason, the Georgics abound in Lucretian echoes.   That does not mean that Virgil copied, however.   Rather Lucretius' poem was a part of Virgil's mind and soul.   He had totally absorbed the language and the ideas of Lucretius so that what he wrote was his own.

It is possible that it took Virgil as long as ten years to write the Georgics. He must have begun the work not long after completing the Eclogues about 37 B.C.   There is reason to believe that he did not put the finishing touches to the poem until 26 B.C.   Tradition reports that the final section of Book IV had originally been a panegyric on Gallus, Virgil's great friend to whom he dedicated the tenth Eclogue; but Gallus fell into disgrace with Augustus, and committed suicide in 26 B.C. —so Virgil had to change that portion. There is no absolute proof for this theory, but it is possible.

Some scholars hold that the Georgics were intended to be propaganda for Augustus' agricultural program, though this is unlikely because Octavius did not adopt the name of Augustus until 27 B.C., by which time Virgil had virtually completed the work.   In addition, Octavius did not become the master of Rome till after the battle of Actium in 31 B.C. when he defeated the forces of Antony and Cleopatra.   (Octavius and Antony had shared the reins of government, on the surface at least, for eleven years.)   During the period

37 to 31 B.C. Octavius may have had grand schemes for revitalizing Italy, but he could not put these into effect before he became supreme. Virgil wrote about the country, not as propaganda for someone else, but because he loved Italy passionately, and believed that the simplicity of country living was a source of Rome's greatness.

The Georgics are dedicated to Virgil's third patron, Maecenas. Virgil says that Maecenas gave him "stern commands" to write on a country topic, but it was probably barely more than a suggestion. Maecenas was certainly in the position to make suggestions: he was an influential statesman who had grouped around him the best writers of his day—Virgil was one, another was the poet Horace. The Georgics consists of four Books on various practical aspects of farming. Much of the advice is still good today. The first book deals with how and when to plant and harvest. The second covers vine and tree growing. The third discusses animals of the farm, and the fourth, how to care for bees. Interspersed with the long sections of instruction are many passages of great beauty. Virgil forever weaves together art and nature in such a way that, though he claims his purpose is to teach (didactic poetry), the actual result is that he inspires (epic poetry).

BOOK I

(LINES 1-42.) Virgil begins the <u>Georgics</u> by telling his patron, Maecenas, the subjects of the four books: farming, and the correct seasons for the various chores of the farmer; tree and vine cultivation; farm animals and their diseases; and how to care for bees. Then he reverently calls upon the gods who are specially fond of these aspects of country life. He refers to the sun and moon as "the bright and shining lights of the universe which lead the gliding year through the sky." Then he mentions Bacchus and Ceres, the goddess of seed-time and harvest. Next he comes to the lesser divinities of the Italian countryside, the Fauns, and the Nymphs of the trees, the Dryads. Then, because he is going to mention animals of the farm, he calls upon Neptune, who gave the horse to man (as well as being the god of the sea). The next divinity mentioned, Aristaeus, was important because he taught men many things about farming, but his particular benefit was showing men how to cultivate bees. (His special place of worship was the island of Ceos in the Aegean Sea.) Naturally, Virgil could not leave out Pan, the shepherd's god, or Minerva, whose gift to men was the olive tree. Then comes the hero who invented the plough, Triptolemus, and after him the god who loved forests in their wild state, Silvanus. The list seems long to us, but Virgil did not want to provoke the anger of any divinity whom he might have left out by mistake, and so he finishes the first portion of his introduction by calling on all the gods and goddesses who have anything to do with farming at all.

The second portion of his introduction is addressed to Octavius. Virgil calls him Caesar because Octavius had adopted that name when he became the heir to the great Julius Caesar. By the time the poet wrote this passage (undoubtedly one of the last, as is the way with introductions), Octavius had become the most important statesman in the known world. In his capacity as ruler of such an enormous empire, he was equal to a god. Virgil even makes a reference to the legend that Venus was the mother of the Julian line. He imagines Octavius as wearing a crown of myrtle which was sacred to Venus. Certainly if the ruler of Rome and the world is not kind to the farmers, they will have no chance of success. All too soon he may be summoned to the underworld, so the poet begs Caesar to be favorable to his rather bold beginning.

> **COMMENT:** Virgil does not begin with an invocation to the gods and to the ruler of Rome because it was the customary and conventional thing to do. Nor is he bowing and scraping in subservience to Octavius. What the poet wants to do is to put the rather lowly subject of farming into an epic setting. Epic is stately and dignified. There is a certain amount of the religious and supernatural in the background. It also contains aspirations of national greatness, personified in a wonderful hero. All these ideas churned in Virgil's mind. So he makes his introduction as lofty as possible.

(LINES 43-159.) After the introduction, the poet turns to the first subject of the book, breaking the ground for planting. When the snow has melted and the sod crumbles easily, it is time for harnessing the oxen to the plough. The land that gives the best yield is land which has been turned under twice, or as Virgil puts it: "has twice felt the sun and twice the cold." (Farmers who believe in mulching may differ with Virgil in some of his precepts, but most of them are still sound today.) But all land is not suitable for every crop, nor is every climate right: Asia Minor produces saffron; India, ivory;

Arabia, frankincense; the Black Sea area, iron and beaver oil; and Epirus, horses. Each product has its own suited place. Another point to remember is that the same piece of ground can not be planted year after year. Every other year it should lie fallow. If there is not enough land to allow this practice, then crops should be rotated. Above all, use manure liberally and then cover it with ashes. If the stubble is very bad, burn it. Use a mattock to break up the hard clods. Golden Ceres smiles on the farmer who is not afraid of hard work.

Pray for warm winters and rainy summers, but if the rains do not come, be ready to irrigate the fields. Yet even the farmer who does his best has to reckon with the pests of nature: cranes, geese, or weeds. Jupiter has not wanted anything to be too easy, "sharpening men's souls with care." In Saturn's Golden Age men did not have to till the lands or set up fences to mark property lines: they gathered the bounty of the earth for a common store. It was Jupiter who brought an end to this paradise. He introduced snakes, took away fire, and made men struggle. "Work conquered all things." Labor omnia vicit is the maxim for farmers! (This is reality indeed, in contrast to the dreamer in the tenth Eclogue who says, "Love conquers all things," omnia vincit amor.) Work is unending, and poverty lurks around the corner.

> **COMMENT:** In this passage Virgil glories work as the salvation for man. This is an interesting concept for the modern world which has placed such emphasis on labor-saving devices. If everything is given us as a free hand-out from the gods, says Virgil, we will become worthless and develop no talents. Conflict, struggle, and overcoming the odds, these develop a mighty people.

NAMES AND PLACES

THULE: possibly Iceland, possibly the coast of Norway, but thought of by the ancients as the furthest land known to man.

TETHYS: mother of the ocean nymphs and of many river gods. Virgil imagines Octavius marrying a sea-nymph, and receiving the kingdom of the ocean as a dowry.

ERIGONE: daughter of Icarius, a mythical Athenian, who had been hospitable to Bacchus. In return Bacchus taught him how to cultivate vines. He was killed by the peasants who drank his wine and thought they had been poisoned when they became drunk. His daughter hung herself in her grief, and Jupiter changed her into the constellation Virgo. Virgo is one of the signs of the Zodiac, along with the Scorpion mentioned in the next line. Virgil imagines the Scorpion drawing in his claws to make room so that Octavius may take his place among the stars.

TARTARUS: the underworld. The Elysian fields were the happy places in the underworld where great heroes went.

PROSERPINA: queen of the underworld, and daughter of Ceres, the goddess of agriculture.

TMOLUS: a mountain in Lydia in Asia Minor.

SABAEANS: a people living in Arabia.

CHALYBES: a people living in Pontus on the Black Sea.

DEUCALION: the only man left alive after the great flood. He and his wife, Pyrrha, (the only woman) were told to throw the bones of their mother behind them in order to repeople the earth. After a while, they figured out that the earth was their "mother" and that all the stones lying around were her "bones."

LETHE: the river of forgetfulness in the underworld.

MYSIA: a district in north-western Asia Minor. Gargarus was located in southern Mysia and noted for being a very fertile region.

(LINES 160-514.) The goddess Ceres was the first to help men grow better crops.   Grain is attacked by pests and blight and weeds. Only constant watchfulness will keep a check on these. And the farmer must know how to use his tools. Virgil here includes a wonderful description of how a plough is made, and the various kinds of wood that go into it.

When it comes to the threshing, the best floor is made of cement, so that mice, moles, weevils, and all the other hundreds of pests can not damage the crop. The farmer can tell by looking at the almond tree whether it will be a good season for grain. If the tree is loaded with blossoms which turn into fruit, it's a good sign; if the tree produces only leaves, the harvest will be scant. A good trick for some seeds, peas and beans especially, is to soak them in soda. This will increase the percentage of germination. It is very important for the farmer to sort out the best seeds for next year's crop, otherwise the stock degenerates.

Man can never relax for a second, for nature takes over so quickly. Everything reverts to its wild stage. This is the law of fate. It is just "as if a man, hardly able to force his way against the current with his oars, should rest his arms for a second. He is swept headlong down-stream."

Now Virgil turns to the seasons and the suitable times of the year for the farmer's various occupations. The farmer, as well as the sailor, must be able to read the stars in the heavens. When the sun is found in the constellation Libra, it is autumn, and time to plough the ground for planting the fall crops, barley, flax, and poppies. In the spring the sun is found in Taurus; then plant beans, millet and clover. When the Pleiades set in the morning (in November), plant grain. Lentils can be sown in the end of October when Arcturus sets. The sun has a fixed path every year in the heavens so that the farmer will know when to do what.

There are many things for the farmer to do if bad weather keeps him indoors. The most important is the care of his tools. He can also brand his herds and tag his bags of grain. He can cut stakes and make baskets. On days sacred to the gods he can still perform tasks to protect his produce and his animals. For example, he can irrigate the fields so the crops do not die from drought; or if his sheep are really suffering from the heat, he can bathe them in the river. And of course on a festival day, the farmer can go to market to sell and to buy.

Just as there are appropriate times of the year for certain activities, there are also special days within the month. The fifth day is bad; the god of the underworld, Orcus, and the Furies, who avenge murders were born on that day. So were the daring giants who tried to make a ladder out of the mountains Pelion, Ossa, and Olympus to get to the sky. The seventeenth day of the month is lucky for planting grape vines, for breaking in a new team of oxen. If you plan to run away, do it on the ninth; but don't steal on that day, for you will surely be caught!

Some tasks are best done at night, or early evening such as cutting stubble or making pine torches. A farmer in Virgil's day would not have had time for television if it had existed! For music he had the sound of his wife's voice as she worked at her weaving or made grape wine. These things can be done at night. But grain must be cut at noon, and then too must the threshing be done. Perhaps it seems as if there would be no end to working. In summer this is pretty true. But in winter, farmers can enjoy the fruits of their hard work. Still, there are some jobs which must be done in the cold weather: picking acorns, laurel-berries, and olives. In the winter the farmer should set his traps for cranes, and nets for deer. "When the snow lies deep and the rivers push ice before them," that is the time for hunting.

Autumn seems to be the time for storms which always come just as the harvest is ready for the reapers. Winds will tear up the crop, laden with its fruit. The stubble will fly over the fields before the black whirlwind. Then follows a description of one of the most wonderful storms in poetry. It is as if we could watch it on a movie screen with a sound track as well. An Egnlish translation can give the picture, but the sounds of long syllables piled one after the other, with lots of m's and s's which are interrupted with sudden short syllables and t sounds — these can not come out in a translation. "Often a mighty column of waters descends from the sky, and clouds gathered together from the depths of heaven, glower and threaten a terrible storm of blackest rain; it is as if the sky itself were falling." In the middle of the blackness, the sudden floods and the terrified oxen, Jupiter stands, lord of all, hurling his thunderbolts. The darkness is torn by lightning. The woods and beaches, lashed by the wind, moan in pain.

Such storms teach man to be humble, to worship the gods, and to offer the best gifts to Ceres: honeycomb and fat young lambs, and mellow wine. Dance in her honor and praise her with hymns. The man who is close to nature can not help being truly religious. If he is in tune with nature, he will read the signs she sends correctly. The farmer can tell when there will be a high wind if he hears a crash of a huge tree on the mountain. Leaves will be lifted up from the ground and start dancing around madly. Nor does rain ever come without first sending a warning. As it moves over the valleys, the cranes fly ahead of it. The heifer will look up and sniff the air. The swallows will fly around nervously. At night the oil lamps will splutter in the damp and the wind.

After a storm, you can see good weather coming. The fog blows away and the stars are bright again. Kingfishers, the pride of the sea-nymph, Thetis, fly out over the water. The mists settle in the valleys. Ravens chatter to each other, glad that the storm is over. It is not that birds and animals have a divine gift of foreknowledge, but that changes in the weather affect them. Everyone knows that if the new moon is surrounded with a misty halo, rain is coming. On the other hand if it rises for four days with clear light, and the tips of its horns quite distinct, the whole month will be free of rain, and sailors too can be thankful. You can also tell if it is going to rain by looking at the sun. When at sunrise the orb seems to be covered with spots and shrinks into the clouds, rain is coming. Or if it is covered by a heavy bank of clouds so that it sends out shafts of light, but the sun itself is almost invisible, then the farmer can expect hail. There are other signs at sunset. If the sun turns blue, it will rain. If it becomes red as fire, a wind storm is coming. If it is a mottled and spotty red, then there will be wind and rain. But if at sunrise and sunset the sun is clear, the farmer need not fear any storm-clouds.

Truly the warnings of the sun are important. For in the year that Julius Caesar was murdered an eclipse of the sun took place (November 44 B.C.). The volcano in Sicily, Aetna, erupted at the same time, and there were many other dreadful portents: beasts spoke, rivers stopped, great yawning caverns opened in the earth. All these terrible signs preceeded another frightful clash of arms. There will come a time when the happy farmer as he ploughs, will turn up javelins, eaten away with rust, or his hoe will clang on empty helmets. And now Virgil is seeing the full horror of war, and he ends this first book about farming on a note of passionate patriotism. "Gods of my native land, Romulus, and mother Vesta, do not prevent this young man from coming to the aid of our war-weary generation. There are too many battles in the world, too many varieties of crime." The world is like a chariot driven by run-away horses which the driver can not control. Let us have peace.

COMMENT: In these closing lines, Virgil with the wondrous skill of the true artist, has raised his book on the precepts of farming to the level of epic poetry. The common facts of weather, sun, moon, and stars, have been elevated by the lofty theme of the need for peace. But perhaps the passage that we remember most vividly is the magnificent storm.

NAMES AND PLACES

KIDS: two stars in Auriga, the charioteer, which rises in April and sets in September, both times of storms.

ABYDOS: a town located on the Hellespont.

ATLAS: the Titan who supported the world on his shoulders was the father of the Pleiades. Maia was one of the Pleiades.

SCYTHIA: in southeastern Europe bordered by the Danube.

RIPHAEAN MOUNTAINS: imaginary mountains marking the northern most spot in Europe. The ancient geographers were never quite agreed as to where they were, and as the territory of the known world increased, the mountains were moved farther and farther north.

STYX: one of the rivers of the underworld.

ATHOS: mountain in the tip of the easternmost peninsula of the three fingers that jut out into the Aegean sea from Macedonia.

RHODOPE: one of the highest mountains in Thrace.

CERAUNIAN MOUNTAINS: extended along the coast of Epirus.

SATURN: the most distant planet known to the ancients.

CYLLENE: the highest mountain in southern Greece, sacred to Mercury. The reference here is to the planet, not the god.

CAYSTER: a river in Lydia in Asia Minor.

SCYLLA AND NISUS: The legend of these two, father and daughter, is given in Eclogue VI, Names and Places. Nisus was later changed into an osprey or sea-eagle, and Scylla into a bird called Ciris. These lines are also found in a poem called Ciris, which most scholars consider to be one of Virgil's earlier works.

GLAUCUS: a sea-divinity.

PANOPEA: a sea-nymph.

MELICERTES: another sea divinity. His mother, Ino, driven mad by the queen of the gods, leapt into the ocean with the boy in her arms. Both mother and son became lesser sea gods.

ERIDANUS: actually more of a river god than a river, since the ancients weren't exactly sure where the river was! It was associated with the

Po because amber was found at its mouth. It is likely that Virgil means the Po here.

ROMULUS: the founder of Rome, according to legend, in 753 B.C.

VESTA: the goddess of the never-dying hearth fire.

LAOMEDON: engaged the sea god, Neptune, and the sun-god, Apollo, to build Troy for him.   When the task was done, he refused to pay his workmen.

SUMMARY: There are many elements in Book I of the Georgics which are reminiscent of the early Greek poet, Hesiod. He wrote a poem called Works and Days. Neither poet actually aimed at writing instructions for farmers. Both wanted to place the seemingly dull routine of farming into the more charming setting of poetry so that they could express their own ideals. Two of Hesiod's ideals, hard work and devotion to the gods, are quite evident in Virgil's book. But the Roman poet's most important theme is his country's need for peace. In contrast to the fourth Eclogue where Virgil is inspired by the idea of a new Golden Age of peace which is at hand, this book ends on a more realistic and sombre note. The poet is older; peace has not yet come. The longing is still there.

BOOK II

(LINES 1-108.) The opening lines are addressed to the god of wine, Bacchus. This is because the subject of the book is how to grow vines and trees. Virgil gives us a wonderfully sensual picture of the god exuberantly wading barelegged through the purple juice of the freshly pressed grapes. After this invigorating introduction, Virgil proceeds in a more steady vein with his subject. There are many ways to grow trees. Some seem to spring up of their own accord in the meadows or along the river bank, such as poplars and willows. Others, such as oaks and chestnuts come up from seeds. Cherries and elms send up slender saplings from the strong root stock. But men have learned how to improve on nature, or at least help her along. Suckers and shoots can be transplanted, and some bushes increase best under the process of layering. Olives can be rooted from just a tiny slip of bark. Apple twigs can be grafted into pear trees with marvelous results. There are many wild fruits and trees which can be improved by cultivation, and this should be a source of great joy to farmers. This will be their great achievement. Then the poet asks his patron, Maecenas, to come with him on the adventurous voyage he is about to undertake. He will not go out over the deep, but will stick close to the shore, as he is not sure that his skill as a poet is great enough. He will be practical, above all.

After this digression where Virgil mentions his patron, he goes back to his subject of grafting and cultivation. The tree that grows wild is not very productive; but if a branch is grafted, or if the suckers are transplanted then the flavor of the fruit and the yield will far surpass what nature could have produced. Hazels, palms, firs and other trees will grow from suckers. Walnuts do well grafted to arbutus, and plane trees can even be the stem for apple branches. In fact almost anything can be done with enough effort. It is important to know the different methods of grafting, for not all methods have equal success for every tree. One method is to make a slit in the knot where the buds push out from the bark. Or in some trees a small hole can be made where there is no knot, and a wedge-shaped shoot can be driven in. Soon a marvelous new tree is stretching toward the sky.

Another thing farmers must know is the fact that there are different varieties within each class of tree. There are all sorts of different olive trees, and at least three kinds of pears. And the varieties of wine are practically number-less. Wine from the island of Lesbos, white wine from lake Mareotis in Egypt, the Falernian from Campania in southern Italy, and many more, all form a wine list that would please any palate. There are more kinds of wine than there are grains of sand in the desert, or waters in the ocean.

The poet has teased us with a taste of wine and now goes back to trees. Not all soils are suitable for every tree. Willows like river banks, the ash loves rock-strewn hillsides. Myrtles grow along the shore; vines like open sunshine. India produces ebony; Ethiopia, cotton, soft as downy wool. The Chinese comb silk from the leaves. (Virgil did not know about the silk worm.) Citron comes from Media, and trees so tall that an arrow can not fly over them grow in India. But nothing these exotic lands offer can possibly equal the praises of Italy. Here there are no bulls that breathe fire, no seeds of dragons' teeth. (Virgil alludes to the legend of Jason, the first great sailor of mythology, who plowed the land of Colchis with fire-breathing bulls, and planted dragons' teeth from which armed men sprang up.) Italy is a land filled to overflowing with fruits and wine and happy herds. In Italy grow the proud war-horse, white oxen, and bulls which lead the processions of a victorious general to the temples of the gods. "Here spring is continuous, and summer lasts into months which are not summer's own." Slowly, slowly, with the subtlety of a magician, Virgil draws his reader from the real world into fairyland. We step imperceptibly from reality into the Golden Age; but we hardly know it has happened. The cattle breed twice a year, and two crops can be picked from the fruit trees. There are no tigers, no lions, no huge scaly serpents. And think of the many glorious cities, and the rivers that glide beneath their walls. How beautiful are the lakes of Italy, Larius (Lake Como) and Benacus (Lake Garda). Man has made the Lucrine lake even more marvelous by cutting a channel through to the sea on one side, and joining it to the lake of Avernus on the other. (These are located near modern Naples. Virgil is paying a tribute to Octavius by mentioning the canal. Octavius' right hand man, Agrippa, had had the canal dug in 37 B.C. so that the two lakes could be a new base for the navy.) Italy also produces silver, copper and gold. But her greatest treasure is the magnificent race of men, inured to hardships through the ages. The names of patriots ring through the generations: Marius, Camillus, Scipio, and last of all Octavius (whom Virgil always called Caesar), leading his triumphal procession through Rome. "Hail great parent of fruitfulness, great mother of men, Saturn's land. It is for thee I start out upon this task and sing the song of Ascra (Hesiod's native town was Ascra) through the Roman towns."

> **COMMENT:** As in Book I, Virgil has started with a humble subject and worked it up to a climax: there the first climax was the passage glorifying work; here it is glorifying Italy. The poet's topic has risen from trees to famous men, to the great Octavius himself, who must become the new founder of the Golden Age. And he names his task at the end of the passage: to make Hesiod's poem, Works and Days, have meaning for Romans of his own day. Virgil is a poet of power and passion as well as delicate sensitivity.

NAMES AND PLACES

LENAEUS: another name for Bacchus coming from a Greek word meaning wine-press.

PARNASSUS: the range of mountains north of Delphi in Greece, sacred to Apollo and the nine Muses.

ISMARUS: a mountain in Thrace which produced grapes that made excellent wine.

TABURNUS: a mountain in southern Italy.

PAPHOS: a town in Cyprus sacred to Venus.

HERCULES: according to legend, the hero found the poplar tree growing on the banks of the Acheron, the river in the underworld, when he went down on his great errand to bring back the monster dog, Cerberus, who guarded the entrance to the lower regions.

CHAONIA: a district in Epirus where there were groves of oaks sacred to Jupiter.

METHYMNA: the second most important city in the island of Lesbos.

ALCINOUS: king of the Phaeacians (Odyssey VII: 112 ff.) He possessed beautiful apple orchards.

THASOS: island in the north Aegaean off the coast of Thrace.

RHAETIA: Roman province south of the Danube.

PHANAE: southern point of the island of Chios. The other names of the various wines are uncertain in origin.

GELONIANS: inhabitants of Scythia.
SERES: unknown people of the far east.
HERMUS: a large river in Asia Minor.
BACTRA: capitol of Bactria, north-west of India.
PANCHAEA: a mythical island near Arabia.
MASSIC: the celebrated wine from the central part of Italy, named after the mountain.
CLITUMNUS: a small river which flows into the Tinia which flows into the Tiber. Its streams were thought to produce the whitest cattle.

(LINES 109-543.) Now Virgil turns to qualities of different soils, and puts his "soil-testing kit" into verse. First comes the nature of soil. A clayey soil is good for olive trees, a rich soil good for vineyards. Good pasture land can be found in Tarentum, or in the land around Mantua which was lost. (Here Virgil alludes to the confiscation of land to pay the veterans of Octavius and Antony.) Black and crumbly earth is good for grain. The thin gravelly soil on a hillside, however, is barely sufficient to support wild herbs on which the bees feed. The best soil of all is the rich, moist land around Capua and on the ridges.

At this point the poet turns to his soil testing. First comes the test for heaviness or lightness. Dig a good sized hole and then put the dirt back in and trample it down. If it sinks below the level of the hole it is light soil, just right for cattle or vineyards; if not, the soil is heavy and will need a plough and oxen to break up the clods. To test the saltiness of the soil, fill a tightly woven basket with it and then pour water through it. Taste the drops that trickle through. They will reveal how salty the soil is. Another way to tell if the soil is rich is to rub it in the fingers. It should have a sticky quality, almost like pitch. It is much harder to detect a cold soil, but if dark ivy and the yew tree are abundant, that is probably fairly indicative.

When it comes to setting out vines, first prepare the trenches. They need not be too deep. Fields where the soil is crumbly are most suitable, though the young twigs can be set out on a sloping hillside also. They should be spaced farther apart however if the ground is not level. And when they are big enough to transplant to their final location, make sure that the same side of the twig is facing the south as it was when growing. This practice gets the new vine off to a strong start. It is a bad idea to have the vineyard slope toward the setting sun. Hazels and olive trees do not make good supporting trees for the vines. Do not graft cultivated olive on wild olive trees, for the cultivated tree burns much more readily than the wild, and sparks from careless shepherds cause tremendous damage. (The poet lets himself go at this point with a marvelous description of an olive grove on fire.)

Never listen to any advice that tells you to plant in the winter. The only time for starting new vines is in the spring. Spring is the season which is helpful to leaves, and to the forests. "In spring the earth starts to swell, and cries out for germinating seeds. Then the almighty father, Sky, descends into the lap of his rejoicing wife with fruitful rains." (Here Virgil has been inspired by a passage from his other great model, Lucretius, I, 250 ff. But Virgil's rain is much more tender. In Lucretius, father sky falls headlong into the lap of mother earth. Virgil thinks that having "father sky" and "mother earth" so close together is too much, and has the sensitivity to allow the reader to understand that the "rejoicing wife" is the earth.) Then follows one of the most lovely descriptions of spring to be found in any language or any poet. It is not sentimental, or overdone. It is filled with life as spring gives life. At the end, it returns from its heights to the earth, the last word in the passage. "Tender green things could not endure this life-giving force if there were not a long period of rest between the cold and warm seasons, and if the indulgence of the sky did not sustain the earth."

And what is the best way to make earth fruitful? Cover it with manure. When the cuttings are set out in this fertile soil, make sure to plant them deep. Surround the roots with a small amount of gravel or shells so that water can seep in and nourish the new plant. After they have started to grow, continue to work the soil with the hoe so that the earth doesn't get packed down hard, and the rain fail to sink in. When they are very tender the only pruning they need can be done with the fingers. Never cut back with a knife until they have established many strong tendrils and encircle the elm on which they are to grow. Even when the vineyard is well established, it will not last long if it is not fenced in by a thick hedge. Animals love to get in and create havoc, cattle, playful goats, and greedy heifers. The goat is probably the worst offender, and that is why the Greeks sacrificed it to Bacchus. (Virgil launches into a brief description as he sees it of the origin of tragedy and comedy. The presenting of plays, or short skits was usually accompanied by the sacrifice of a goat in honor of Bacchus.) It is always important for the farmer to remember the gods.

When the vines are full grown, the struggle to keep them healthy and productive goes on throughout the year. The soil must be worked continuously to keep it from becoming packed down. Growing vines need constant pruning. Brambles must be weeded out. Reeds must be cut by the river with which to tie the vines to their parent trees. In truth, the farmer does well to just admire the big estates, and stick to cultivating only small farms. Just when he thinks his work is done, and he will harvest bushels and bushels of grapes, they may be utterly ruined by a heavy down-pour. Well may he curse himself for not picking the grapes yesterday. Virgil does not say all this, but he hints at the frustration of the hard-working farmer who can never relax for a minute.

Olives, however, are another matter. They require virtually no care at all. Fruit trees, too, are easy. (Apparently it wasn't necessary to spray in those days. The balance of nature took care of the insect pests most of the time.) There are many wild fruits and berries which grow without the help of man. There is beauty in uncultivated fields, and trees which grow wild have their usefulness. Pine trees are used for ships; cedars and cypresses for houses. Farmers use them for spokes and wheels for their heavy wagons, too. Myrtle is used for spears; yew for bows. Linden and box are good for carving. Bees make their hives in hollow ilex trees. What can the vine do in comparison with these innumerable uses of trees?

Oh how lucky, how truly lucky is the farmer who is aware of his blessings. (Virgil can stick to the careful particulars of agriculture only so long before his poetic inspiration must soar higher to a more general theme.) Far from war, the earth pours forth her sustenance for him. He does not need to join the throng of hangers-on who crowd around the mansions of the wealthy, hoping for some sort of a hand-out. He may never get a chance to see doors inlaid with tortoise-shell, or clothes enbroidered with gold, or white wool dyed purple. But his pleasures are more lasting, and richer. Richer by far are the cool caves, the living lakes, the sheltered valleys, and the mooing cattle. Farmers worship the gods from their hearts. It is not empty ceremony to them. Justice left her last footprint among the simple country-folk when she disappeared from the earth at the end of the Golden Age.

Now the poet intrudes his own philosophy, which grew out of the assimilation of his beloved model, Lucretius, with his own inner longings. Happy is the man who knows the causes of things, he says, referring to Lucretius. Happy also is the man who is able to enjoy the country and learn its lessons, referring to his own love. It would be wonderful to understand the stars in their courses, the eclipses of the sun and moon, the reasons for earthquakes, or what makes twilight. But perhaps I am not brilliant enough, he says, to be able to understand. At least my joy can be in the rivers and the valleys of the country.

Now he leaves the first person to make this other type of love apply to anyone. The man who loves the country and its woodland gods knows no ups and downs of kingdoms or the mad pace of the Forum (the Wall Street of Rome, almost). Others explore the seas, wage wars and destroy kingdoms to gain extravagant wealth. He is not swayed by smooth-tongued politicians. He does not murder to get his brother's inheritance, and end up an exile under a foreign sun. It is true that he knows no rest, that the struggle never ends. But his reward is the abundant harvest, the increasing size of the herd, and bursting barns. And the tranquility of his home is undisturbed, (no nervous breakdowns, no psychiatrists, no divorces, no ulcers). His children run to greet him with kisses, and on holidays the master of the house fills, and fills again, the merry wine bowl. Everyone carouses happily on the green grass or vies with each other in games and races.

This is the sort of life the early primitive tribes in Italy enjoyed. From such a hardy life came the mighty men who made Rome. (Doesn't it remind the modern reader of our hardy ancestors who conquered the west with their endurance and initiative?) Then in a twinkling, we have stepped through the glass door into the Golden Age again. In the reign of Saturn war was unknown, with its piercing bugle calls and the clang of the anvil. "But we have completed a voyage over tremendous spaces; it is time now to unharness our foaming horses." And Book II leaves us in the happy days of the Golden Age.

COMMENT: The book ends, not despondently as did Book I, but on a high note of philosophy. What seems to be a manual for the man who would plant a vineyard, turns out to be a manual for the man who would find true contentment. Virgil's farmer is happy, not because he has no need to work, but because the results of his work are rewarding to his soul.

NAMES AND PLACES

CLANIUS: river in southern Italy which often flooded the town, Acerrae, on its banks.

LYAEUS: another name for Bacchus (from a Greek word meaning release from care).

THESEUS: the first king of Athens to incorporate Attica under his rule. As a young man he rescued the Athenian boys and girls who had been sent to the king of Crete as tribute. Athens was the site of the great Dionysiac festivals at which tragedy originated. (Dionysus is the Greek name for

Bacchus.)   Virgil also alludes to the rural Dionysia which he thinks of as being the origin of comedy.

AUSONIA: another name for Italy, found frequently in the Aeneid. It is derived from the name of a tribe, Ausones, who lived in south-central Italy.

CYTORUS: a mountain in the northern section of Asia Minor.

NARYX: a town in Locris in Greece. Locris was reputed to be the mother country of the inhabitants of Bruttium in southern Italy. Bruttium supported large stands of pines.

ITURAEANS: a tribe of Arabian archers in Palestine.

CENTAURS: Bacchus is held responsible for the quarrel which broke out between the Lapiths and Centaurs (mythical peoples) at the marriage feast of the Lapith's king, Pirithoüs.   It was Bacchus' fault that they all became drunk.

EPHYRA: old name for Corinth.

SPERCHEUS: a river in the south of Thessaly.

TAYGETUS: a high range of mountains near Sparta in southern Greece.

HAEMUS: a range of mountains in Thrace.

ROSTRA: the speaker's platform in the Forum.   The benches mentioned in the next sentence refer to the theatre where the people would clap loudly for the prominent politicians when they entered.

SICYON: a district in Greece on the southern shore of the Gulf of Corinth.

SUMMARY: There is a certain similarity between Books I and II in the way they were composed. Both commence with introductions and invocations to the proper gods. Both work up to two high points which close with passages of glorious poetry. There are several contrasts, however.

1.   Where the first book uses the professor-poet Hesiod as a model, the second uses the philosopher-poet Lucretius. At the end of Book II, however, Virgil has returned to Hesiod by ending with the Golden Age, the point at which Hesiod's poem, Works and Days, begins.

2.   The two subjects of Book I, farming and weather, are separated, one occupying the first half, and the other, the second half of the book. But the two subjects of Book II, tree and vine cultivation, are twined together much the way the vine actually twines around its tree for support.

3.   Perhaps the most important difference is the one more deeply related to the purpose of the whole poem. Book I is a national appeal with a strongly expressed feeling of patriotism in a desperate need for peace.   Book II ends on a note of appeal to the individual to look for happiness in the right places. No wonder Virgil fitted so well into the religious atmosphere of the Middle Ages.

BOOK III

(LINES 1-48.) This book commences on an epic note. Virgil proclaims that he will sing a theme so noble, so lofty, that his name will fly from mouth to mouth throughout the earth. He will return to his native Mantua and set up a temple to Octavius. He himself will be dressed like a victor in purple, and drive a hundred four-horse chariots. Scenes of war, the people of the Ganges submitting to the Romans, naval battles on the Nile with the ships' beaks lined up in rows, will be carved on the gold and ivory doors of this temple. There will be statues of the Trojan ancestor, Assaracus, and a statue of Apollo since he and the sea-god, Neptune, built Troy. And the enemies of Octavius shall be pictured, trembling in the underworld before the vengeance of the Furies, and enduring the tortures of the damned. Such will be Virgil's lofty themes in the future. Now he still has the wishes of his patron, Maecenas, to fulfill, although he burns to sing of Octavius' battles.

COMMENT: This is a rather lengthy introduction with apparently little bearing on the subject, the animals of the farm. But Virgil has set himself a challenge, a challenge which pursued him all through his poetry: to write an epic equal to that of his most famous predecessors, the Greek Homer, and the Roman Ennius. The temple in this passage symbolizes the epic he has in mind. In these lines he prophesies the writing of the Aeneid. When he finally wrote the great epic, however, some of his earlier concepts had changed. Although Octavius was always in the back of his mind, he picked a mythical, and thus more universal hero, Aeneas. The picture of the underworld occurs in Book VI of the Aeneid, but it is not just a place for torturing Octavius' enemies. Virgil uses it to create a procession of the events of Roman history. For as he grew older, the poet's theme of the mission of Rome to bring peace became broader and deeper.

NAMES AND PLACES

PALES: a Roman goddess of flocks and shepherds.

AMPHRYSUS: a river in Thessaly. When Apollo was banished from Olympus, he went to tend the flocks of the king of Thessaly, Admetus, along the banks of this river. Thus the shepherd of Amphrysus is Apollo.

LYCAEUS: a mountain in Arcadia in Greece, sacred to Pan. Virgil invokes here Pales, Apollo and Pan.

EURYSTHEUS: the king of Tiryns in Greece who set Hercules to perform the famous twelve labors.

BUSIRIS: a king of Egypt who sacrificed all strangers that came to his country, all that is except Hercules, who killed him.

HYLAS: a youth whom Hercules loved. He was so beautiful that the nymphs of a fountain dragged him down to live with them.

LATONA: the mother of the twin gods, Apollo and Diana. She gave birth to them on the island of Delos.

HIPPODAME: daughter of the king of Pisa in Elis, Greece. The king, Oenomaus, had learned that he would be murdered by his son-in-law. The only way to prevent that was to prevent Hippodame from getting married. So he declared that anyone who wanted his daughter's hand would have to beat him in a chariot race. Since his horses were the fastest in the world, no one had any luck. No one, that is, until Pelops came along. He bribed the king's charioteer to take out the lynch pins from the wheels of the king's chariot. He also had the divine aid of Neptune's horses and gold chariot. In the race, Oenomaus' chariot broke down, of course, and Pelops won. In mentioning all these names, Virgil is alluding to the practice, common among poets of his day, of filling the pages of their verse with obscure legends.

AONIA: a section of Boeotia in Greece where Mt. Helicon was located. Mt. Helicon was one of the homes of the Muses.

IDUMAEA: southern part of Judea.

ALPHEUS: a river in Greece, flowing through Arcadia and Elis and falling into the sea near Olympia. Near it the Olympian games were held.

MOLORCHUS: a shepherd who entertained Hercules in the Nemean groves, near Argos in southern Greece. It was also the site of the Nemean games. Virgil is saying that the games in honor of Octavius will be greater than the Olympian or Nemean games of Greece. These words are symbolic of Virgil's goal, to surpass the epics of the Greeks.

NIPHATES: a mountain in Armenia.

ASSARACUS: the genealogy is as follows: Jupiter, Teucer, Dardanus, Erichthonius, Tros, Assaracus.

CYNTHIUS: means Apollo from the mountain Cynthus on the island of Delos.

COCYTUS: a river in the underworld.

IXION: was chained to a wheel by his hands and feet. This wheel never stopped turning in the underworld. The stone mentioned next was the punishment of Sisyphus. He had to keep rolling a huge block of marble up a hill only to have it roll down again.

DRYADS: nymphs of the trees.

CITHAERON, TAYGETUS, EPIDAURUS: Virgil uses these names to announce his subject of animals. The first was a mountain in Boeotia where game was plentiful. Taygetus was a mountain in Sparta famous for its hunting dogs. Epidaurus, a town near Argos in Greece, was famed for its temple to the god of healing, Aesculepius. Also, according to Virgil, it produced famous horses.

TITHONUS: a prince of Troy, and brother of the king of Troy, Priam.

After the introduction of fifty lines, Virgil begins with his main topic. First he discusses breeding cattle, and then horses. A good cow looks fierce, has an ugly head, and a thick neck. You can tell a good horse by the way he prances, holds his head, and tosses his mane. (Then he names some of the famous horses of antiquity. He also alludes to the myth where Saturn changed himself and his amour of the moment into horses to escape the anger of his wife, Rhea.) When the stallion grows old, however, he must be turned out. A horse must have youth and strength. Look at the horses in the chariot racing. The Lapiths were the first to make bridles and bits, and to train the horse to follow man's command. The most spirited horse can well claim ancestry from the god Neptune, the horse-tamer.

When the farmer has selected his stallion, then he must feed him well. Grass which is in flower, water, and grain are most important. But mares must be thin so that they will be more ready to mate. It is sometimes a good idea to get them completely tired out to enable conception to take place. The pregnant mare should then be the farmer's chief concern. They should be allowed to feed in the open groves and beside the rivers where the grass is greenest. Above all, they should be protected from the terrible fly whose sting maddens horses. The poet refers to the story of Io, daughter of Inachus, to illustrate the fury of the gadfly. She was loved by Jupiter, but he changed her into a heifer, on account of Juno's jealousy. The queen of the gods then invented the gadfly to pursue her and make her miserable. Virgil has been talking about horses, but makes his illustration with the story of a cow, so that readers will be aware of the fact that he knows the gadfly hurts both.

Now the subject passes to the care of new-born calves. First they must be branded, and then a decision made as to whether the calf should be set aside for breeding purposes, kept as a sacrificial animal, or trained to bear the yoke. If the last, remember to be gentle at first and make the first yoke out of light osiers. Later when they are trained, you can yoke them to a heavy axle with brass bound poles. Their mother's milk should be saved for them alone when they are small. In that way they will grow to be strong.

The same care goes for foals. If he is to be a war horse, hang bells in his stall to get him used to noise. And when training begins, the most important thing is words of encouragement and praise. Not till the third summer has passed should you attempt to teach him paces. Then you will find that he is as swift as the north wind driving rain storms before it. But to get the best out of either horses or cattle, keep them separated from the opposite sex. Otherwise you will find your best bulls fighting over some heifer and wasting all their strength. Then follows a vivid picture of the beaten bull.

Suddenly the poet has come upon the subject of love, mostly love among the birds and beasts, to be sure, though one young man creeps into the picture. The young man is the hero, Leander, who swam the Hellespont to reach his love. For the rest, Virgil makes poetry out of the lust of animals. It is quite a feat! Only when the lioness is filled with desire does she forget her mother instincts. When a stallion gets the scent of a mare on the wind he becomes uncontrollable. The boar paws the ground, throwing up great piles of dirt, and rubs his side against the trees. As for mares, they are particularly inspired by Venus: she drove the mares of Glaucus mad when he would not let them breed, and they devoured him.

But on to the next topic, says the poet: the smaller animals of the farm. The first thing to remember is to keep the sheep in their pens with plenty to eat there until summer has returned. Make sure the hard ground is covered with straw and ferns to keep away the cold, and to prevent them from getting foot rot. Passing to goats, they thrive on water and arbutus, if their winter pens face the south. Sheep are valuable for their wool which can be dyed purple and bring a high price. But goats are just as valuable for their wonderful foaming milk. When summer finally comes, both sheep and goats can be put out to pasture at daybreak. By ten o'clock they are probably very thirsty, so let them drink from the wells, or ponds or oaken troughs. In the burning heat of noon, they should be encouraged to seek the shade of Jupiter's oak trees or the groves of ilex. In the afternoon, water them again, and when the evening star is rising, or the new moon, drive them back to the folds. Of course, different lands have different methods for caring for their flocks. In Libya the shepherds are nomads, and the sheep roam the open, day and night. The Scythian shepherds who tend their flocks by lake Maeotis and the Danube foaming with yellow sand, have to keep their flocks in the pens all year long because of the terrible cold. Winter in that land is unbelievable. Ice forms over the rushing water of the river. Even wine turns to ice and has to be cracked with an ax. Deer are easy to hunt because they freeze where they stand. The men themselves live in caves dug very deeply, and while away the winter drinking bitter wine.

That is the life of the Scythian shepherd. But the Italian farmer or shepherd who wants good wool must not let his sheep feed where there are briars or burs. The sheep with the whitest fleece are best, although if a ram has a black tongue, for all the whiteness of his fleece, he will be worthless as a breeder. His offspring will have spotted coats. There is nothing so lovely as snowy wool. With it Pan persuaded the moon to follow him.

If milk is the more important product, feed the flocks on lotus and clover -Virgil has now switched to goats. If the goats are milked in the morning, the farmer can make cheese from it in the evening. There are two kinds of cheese, the one for home use, and the other to be stored and sold in the market. The farmer should also remember to care for his dogs. Spartan and Mollosian hounds thrive on whey. They will protect the farm from brigands and wild animals, and they are essential for hunting.

Another important factor in raising sheep and goats is to be on the watch for pests and diseases. Water-snakes, vipers, and aders often slither into the pens undetected. The best way to prevent this is to keep the stalls absolutely clean. If a snake appears, throw rocks or sticks at its head when it is about to strike. The water-snake is no bother as long as the rivers are full. But when the stream beds dry up, and the parched ground cracks with heat, then he glides over the field with his three-forked tongue ready to strike. Diseases of the flocks cause equal damage. If the sheep are drenched by a sudden shower, or too chilled by winter, scab may develop. Sometimes patches of sweat do not get completely washed off, or cuts from the briars are not thoroughly cleansed. That is why it is a good idea to bathe the flock thoroughly. Also, when the sheep have been sheared, the shepherd can treat the skin-sores with the dregs of olive oil, mixed with the scum which forms on top of silver when it is melted, and sulphur. Add to this pitch, oily wax, sea onions, hellebore, (the root of a lily-like plant with a dreadful smell) and black bitumen. If that doesn't work, a remedy that never fails is to lance the head of the ulcerous sore. It the fever spreads in spite of these precautions, open a vein in the foot to let the blood flow. The shepherd can tell if a sheep is stricken with the disease because of its listless behavior. Such a sheep will take no interest in the cropping of grass, but will seek the shade and lag behind the rest of the flock. Sometimes it is advisable to kill the sick sheep, for disease among animals spreads like wild-fire.

Even now you can see the effects of the terrible plague that struck down the flocks along the banks of the Timavus river in northern Italy. Dogs as well as cattle, sickened and died. Their necks swelled and they choked to death, or they broke out in a terrible sweat. In anguish their flanks heaved as they tried to draw their painful breath. Steers would drop dead as they were pulling the plow, and the farmer would sadly unyoke the steer that remained alive. What was the use of the poor animal's toil? He never joined in excessive revels such as men when they are drunk. His food was leaves and simple grass; his wine, the clear running water. (There is a certain pathos in this scene. Virgil is not being sentimental, for he knows that every farmer suffers when he looses one of his animals.)

When the animals had perished, men had to till the fields themselves with harrows or their own nails. But the farmer had no worries from wolves or snakes, for all the wild creatures were dying too. Birds plummeted from the sky, and the hills echoed with the constant bleating of sheep and lowing of dying cattle. In the stalls bodies were piled on bodies, as the dead out-numbered the living. The hides were useless, and even if it had been possible to shear the pus-covered fleece, the disease would have eaten out his stricken limbs. And as horror mounts upon horror, the third Georgic comes suddenly to a halt.

> COMMENT: The last section of this book is reminiscent of the closing passage of Lucretius' On the Nature of Things. The earlier poet describes the horrors of the plague to man, while Virgil, in keeping with his book on farming, paints the dying agonies of sheep and cattle. It seems a rather gruesome climax with which to end the book, but it leaves the reader with the hidden warning, perhaps, that man is not always the master of his fate.

NAMES AND PLACES

POLLUX: and Castor were twin heroes, born in Amyclae in Laconia in southern Greece. They were famous for their skill in taming horses.

ACHILLES: the great Greek hero, in the Trojan war. His horses were Xanthus and Balius. (See Homer's Iliad, XVI, 148.)

ERICHTHONIUS: a mythological king of Athens, who later became the constellation of Auriga, the Charioteer, because he was the first to yoke four horses to a chariot.

LAPITHS: a mythical people living in the mountains of Thessaly.

SILARUS: a river in Italy north of the mountain Alburnus.

TANAGER: a tributary of the Silarus.

PISA: a city in Elis in Greece near where the Olympian games took place. Close by was a grove sacred to Jupiter called Altis.

BELGIAN CHARIOTS: were really British chariots, according to Julius Caesar (Gallic Wars, IV, 33.) They were adopted by wealthy Romans, and Virgil is probably thinking of well-bred carriage horses.

SILA: a range of mountains in southern Italy.

BACCHUS: the wine-god, wandered through Asia and India teaching men the use of the wine. His chariot was drawn by lynxes and tigers.

GARGARUS: the southern portion of Mt. Ida near Troy.

ASCANIUS: a lake in Bithynia.

CASTALIA: a spring on Mt. Parnassus near Delphi in Greece.

CINYPS: a river in Libya famous for its breed of long-haired goats.

MOLOSSI: a tribe who lived in Epirus and bred fierce dogs.

CALABRIA: the southeast peninsula of Italy.

BISALTAE: a tribe in Thrace.

GELONI: a Scythian tribe.

GETAE: people living in the north-east portion of Thrace.

NORICUM: the country between the Danube and the Alps.

CHIRON AND MELAMPUS: are symbolic of the art of healing which has no effect against the plague. This line is reminiscent of a line in Lucretius: "Medicine had to keep silence through fear." (VI, 1179.)

TISIPHONE: one of the terrible Furies. She figures prominently in the Aeneid. Here she personifies the punishment of the gods for sin.

SUMMARY: Book III is considerably different from the first two. It has no outstanding passages of beautiful poetry which could be cut out and pasted in an anthology. In this book, the poet keeps entirely to his subject, after the rather long and startling introduction. The two passages where he elaborates a little are those on love and disease among animals. There are, however, a number of references to mythology which add a flavor of epic to this otherwise very down-to-earth book.

BOOK IV

(LINES 1-87.) The first lines of Book IV are a brief introduction. Virgil will discuss the heavenly gift of honey. His patron, Maecenas is in favor of the subject. The life of bees, their battles, their labor, are on a tiny scale, but if the poet fulfills his task well, his glory will be not so slight. Lastly, he asks Apollo to preside over his efforts.

The first thing the bee-keeper must do is find a safe home for the hive out of the reach of the wind. It should be located as far from where sheep and goats are apt to go as possible. They will trample all over the flowers, or knock the dew off the blades of grass. Birds and lizards are the enemies of bees too. A shady spot near springs or a pool is the best place. Then when the kings lead out the swarms of young in the spring-time they will find pleasant shade from the heat. Plant cassia (an herb of the pea family) and thyme with its pervasive fragance, and savory, and "let violets drink from the over-flowing spring." (It doesn't take much imagination to see, feel and smell this cool and inviting place.)

Having settled the location of the hive, the next step is its construction. It can be made of either hollow bark, or woven of osiers, but it is important to make its entrances small. Otherwise the cold will freeze the honey in winter, and in summer the heat melt it. Either event would be a dreadful calamity for the bees, as they work so hard filling up the crannies with wax or gluey substance made from the pollen of flowers. And don't let yew trees grow near the hive, or roast crabs where the smoke can reach the bees. And never place the hive in a muddy location or in a spot that echoes. Bees are extraordinarily sensitive creatures. When summer comes they will take to the woods and gather pollen from the purple flowers. If the keeper wants them to return, he must spread about perfumes which the bees like, and make a clanging sound by clashing the cymbols of the Great Mother, Cybele. (Virgil is using very grand language for bees. He wants to make a miniature epic of the life of these tiny creatures.) Then they will come back of their own accord.

Sometimes the bees go forth to war because of rival kings. Then the trumpets sound and they all flock together, and make ready their stings. High up into the air the noise of the battle goes. The two armies are massed in one huge ball. Some tumble headlong like thick hail, or a shower of acorns from an oak tree. The chiefs have glorious wings and within their tiny breast their great souls beat, determined to win. But this mighty war and strife a few handfuls of dust, thrown up into the air, can bring to an end.

> **COMMENT:** The reader must not ask if everything Virgil writes is true. The poet doesn't seem to be aware that there is no such thing as a king bee. Still, he is writing epic, and perhaps there is a bit of satire aimed at man in the grand phrases with which he discusses the habits of bees.

(LINES 88-228.) When the battle is over, the bee-keeper should be sure to kill the king which was defeated, if his rival did not kill him. He will only be a source of trouble. The bees whose color is brightest will make the best honey and be the best workers. Rid your hive of the others. Don't let the bees swarm aimlessly in the sky. It is easy to keep them from doing this by clipping the wings of the king. If he can not fight, the other bees will not either. Make sure there are gardens of fragrant saffron flowers around, protected from the birds by the master scarecrow himself, Priapus. As the poet dwells upon the thought of the garden, he goes off on a tangent describing some other enchanting ones. He cannot bear not to mention the rose-gardens of Paestum which bloom twice a year. He loves the rows of endive along the stream, the rich green of parsley, and the squash vine winding along the ground. How beautiful are the late-blooming narcissus, ivy and myrtle. He remembers when he spent some time in Tarentum (founded by a mythical king of Sparta, Oebalus), near the Galaesus river. There a man who had spent most of his life as a pirate was able to turn a few acres of what looked like most unproductive land into a fabulous garden filled with lilies, poppies and other delicacies. "He was the first to pluck the roses in the spring and the apples in the fall". He was able to make hyacinths bloom in the middle of winter. Because of these abundant flowers, he had the best swarm of bees. His fruit trees were a mass of blossoms in the spring, and in the fall there were as many fruits as there had been flowers. (That is really quite a miracle.) He is a genius at grafting too. He could make the wild black-thorn produce domesticated plums. The poet could go on for pages, he is so carried away with this wonder-filled garden. But he checks himself and goes back to his theme of bees. He got onto the subject of gardens because the Cilician pirate had such a good hive.

Jupiter, the king of the gods, has given marvelous qualities to the bees because they fed him when he was hiding from his father Saturn on the island of Crete. (Saturn knew that one of his children would depose him, so he ate each one as it was born. But Jupiter's mother managed to get him away to a cave on Mt. Dicte in Crete. When the baby cried, the Cretan priests clashed their cymbols to drown out the noise.) The bees practice a communism that truly works: they have children in common, common dwellings, and live according to great laws. They work hard together all summer in preparation for the coming winter, gathering everything into a common store. Some look after the finding of food, some work in the fields, some work in the hive, some bring up the young, and some pack the honey. Their perfect division of labor produces the liquid nectar, sweet with the fragrance of thyme. The energy the tiny things expend is as great as the energy of the giant Cyclops. These one-eyed monsters work the huge furnaces under the volcano, Aetna, in Sicily. (Virgil later takes this description of the Cyclopes at work at their forge over into the Aeneid. There the giants make Aeneas' divine armor.) But to continue with the division of labor: the aged build the hives while the young carry home the pollen. They all rest at the same time and work at the same time - in the morning they swarm out of the hive together, in the evening they all return. For a while they buzz around the entrance, but soon all is quiet for the night. If it looks like rain, they stay close to home and only make short forays out to the nearby fields. If it is very windy (and this is more picturesque than true) they pick up tiny stones as ballast to keep them from being buffeted around.

Their method of propagation is nothing short of miraculous. (Virgil does not seem to know that the queen bee is the one who produces the eggs.) They do not have intercourse or waste their strength in love-making, or endure the pains of child-birth. Instead they find the young on the leaves of herbs and carry them to the hive in their mouths. But as easily as they come into the world, just as easily do they leave it, dying willingly out in the fields under their loads. They obey the king bee as if he were a monarch more absolute than a eastern potentate. If they loose him, they give up the hive altogether.

Virgil's emphasis on the allegiance to the non-existent king bee does make a nice epic touch.

It is because of these wonderful characteristics that some people believe that the bees partake of a share of the divine spirit which permeates the universe. For these philosophers hold that "God goes through everything, the lands, the paths of the sea, and the heavens. From him flocks, herds, men, and every kind of wild beast summon their tenuous lives as they are born. And doubtless to him they all return; nor is there a place for death but, still living, they fly among the number of the stars and mount to the depths of heaven."

> **COMMENT:** By the end of the first section of the book the poet has raised us to the heights of religious philosophy. For Virgil, religion and philosophy were almost one and the same thing, but he is torn between two concepts. The first is the philosophy of Epicurus (342-271 B.C.), which Lucretius followed in his On the Nature of Things: all things in the universe are the result of the way atoms fall together. The gods live a life set apart from that of men, and have nothing to do with them. Virgil seems to expound this philosophy in the first Georgic where he says that no divine inspiration makes animals and birds prophets of the weather, but they respond from instinct. But the fourth Georgic seems to contain elements of the second concept, the opposite philosophy of the Stoics. (Zeno, the founder of this philosophy lived around 335 to 263 B.C.) There is a divine spirit which moves in all things. The poet, with his profound religious feelings seems more and more to incline to the latter philosophy, but the passage does not necessarily prove that he believed in the immortality of the soul.

(LINES 229-566.) Now Virgil tells how to get the honey without being stung. Carry a smoking torch in front of you to stun them or drive them away, for when maddened, their stings are poisonous. Honey can be collected twice a year, at the times when the constellation of the Pleiades rises (in May) and when the constellation sets (in November). Even if you think the winter will be severe, and that some honey should be left for the bees themselves, you should still gather it. Otherwise pests, such as salamanders, beetles, or hornets will get what you leave. The more you take of the bees' honey, the harder they will work to restore it.

Bees have ills, as well as man. As they become sick they change color, and get thin. They flit around the entrance to the hive listlessly, and their buzzing has a peculiar sound, like the south wind sighing in the trees. Sometimes the keeper can arouse their spirits by burning aromatic gum, or feeding them honey on the ends of long reeds. There is a purple flower of the aster family which grows in the meadows, very bitter to the taste. Simmer the roots in wine and set the concoction in baskets before the openings of the hive. This remedy may work. But if the whole hive dies out, then try the experiment of the Arcadian bee-keeper, Aristaeus: kill a young bull-calf by stopping its nostrils and mouth and beating it to death. The flesh should be pounded, but the hide should be left whole. Leave the animal in a tiny hut which is quite dark except for four small windows in each wall. Strew about thyme and other sweet smelling herbs and branches. Soon, if these instructions are followed in the beginning of spring, you will find buzzing creatures emerge, and the swarm will burst forth like a shower from summer clouds.

This passage marks the end of instructions and the beginning of the wonderful epic-myth of how Aristaeus learned to create a new swarm. Long ago in the vale of Tempe, by the river Peneus, Aristaeus stood weeping. He had lost his bees through sickness and hunger. The young man complained bitterly to his mother. "Oh mother Cyrene, nymph of this river, why ever did you bring me forth into this hateful world. Why don't you tear up my trees, and burn my crops and my stalls, or chop down my wines, if I am so hateful to you?"

His mother was sitting at the bottom of the stream, chatting with her sister Nymphs. One of them, Arethusa, called her attention to the loud weeping that was going on and said, "Oh sister, Cyrene, your dearest care, your Aristaeus is berating you for your cruelty." So the mother, pierced by his sad cries, told Arethusa to bring her son to him. The youth wandered around marveling at the watery home till he came to his mother's chamber. She listened to his sad tale while her sister Nymphs bathed his hands and brought out napkins and filled the table with a feast. Cyrene poured out a libation three times to Ocean with clear ambrosia. Then she gave a long answer to her son.

"In the Carpathian sea, far, far away, there dwells an old sea-monster, Proteus. Blue-green in color is he, and his chariot is drawn by fishes and a team of two-footed sea-horses. Every so often he revisits his native home in Thessaly. We Nymphs all honor him, and so does the sea-god, Nereus. He has great knowledge of both past and future. You, my son, must go and bind him while he is sleeping so that when he wakes you may question him. Never will he tell you anything of his own free will. You must force him. Even when you have bound him, he will try to escape by changing his shape to scare you. He will become a boar, a tiger, a serpent, or a roaring lioness. But hold him fast till he returns to his own shape. Then he will counsel you."

The beautiful Nymph then poured fragrant ambrosia over her son, and strength and suppleness flowed in his veins. Then she led him to the entrance of Proteus' cave and concealed him there. She went off a short distance to watch. It was the season of terrible heat, when the Dog-Star blazed, and the grass withered, and the rivers dried in their beds. Proteus came out of the waves, looking for his favorite cave. All around him the beasts of the sea frolicked, reminding one of a shepherd followed by his playful flock at evening. Barely had the old god closed one eye when Aristaeus had him tied securely. The wizard went through his repertoire of shapes, including fire, beasts, and water, to no avail. Aristaeus held fast. Finally Proteus gave up, saying: "Look here, young man, whose idea was it for you to invade my home?" And Aristaeus answered him boldly: "You know perfectly well, Proteus. No one can deceive you. I would like an oracle, please." The gray-green eyes of the blue-green wizard flashed. He gnashed his teeth in frustration, but he gave an answer at last.

"Your troubles are due to the sorrow and rage of Orpheus, weeping for his lost bride, Eurydice, killed by the bite of a water-snake. Her Dryad sisters mourned her, roaming over the great mountains of the world. And Orpheus was inconsolable. Day in day out, year in year out, he sang of his love accompanying himself on his lyre. So beautiful was his music that he charmed the ghosts of the underworld, like flocks of migrating birds, as he went down in search of the woman he loved. Even the avenging Furies with their snakey tresses were spell-bound. Proserpina, the queen of the under-world, granted his wish, and he retracted his steps with dear Eurydice following close behind. They were just about to step into the upper world, when Orpheus, forgetting the expressed command of Proserpina not to look back, turned around to see if Eurydice were still there. 'Oh Foolish Orpheus,' she cried, 'now you have lost me forever. I will be wrapped in endless night, stretching out my weak hands to you in vain.' So saying, she vanished like smoke into thin air. Now indeed there was no hope for him, no place to go, no prayers to pray. The sad strains of his song charmed oak trees and tigers, sadder even than the song of a nightingale which has lost her young when a farmer robs her nest. No power on earth could change his sadness, not even the merry sound of a wedding-song. Alone he wandered through all the cold regions of the north and Thrace. Finally one day, the women of the Cicone tribe in that country, exasperated by such unnecessary devotion, tore Orpheus limb from limb, and strewed his remains over the fields. But the Hebrus river, with a father's care, flooded its banks and carried away the bodiless head, still beautiful in death. And forever after the voice of Orpheus has sounded from the banks, 'Eurydice, Eurydice, Eurydice.' "

In a flash the wizard lept into the sea, and left only a whirlpool behind him. Aristaeus was still confused, not quite understanding what the tale of Orpheus had to do with him. But his dear Nymph-mother knew. "My son," she said, "take heart. It is the Nymphs who were Eurydice's playmates, who have brought this trouble on your bees. You must try to appease them. Pick out four of the most perfect bulls from your herds which graze on Mt. Lycaeus, and as many heifers. Then make four altars and drain the blood from the animals' throats, but leave their bodies in the leafy grove. When rosy-fingered dawn has come for the ninth time, consecrate poppies to the ghost of Orpheus, and sacrifice a black sheep. Then go back to the grove and kill a calf for Eurydice. All will be well."

Aristaeus immediately set about to fulfill his mother's commands. Everything turned out as she had said. But on the ninth day a wondrous miracle took place. For swarming all over the rotting animals were clouds and clouds of bees.

So ends the fairy-tale adventures of Aristaeus, and the poet has brought us through the cycle of loss of bees to finding them again. His work is finished.

While Octavius progressed in triumph through the east, establishing the laws of the victor, Virgil was occupied at Naples with a task not nearly so great. (He uses the name Parthenope because she was one of the Sirens who was buried there.) "I toyed with songs of shepherds and, daring in my youth, I sang of you, Tityrus, under the shade of a beech tree." This last line of the fourth Georgic is the same as the first line of the first Eclogue except for one word, the verb sing. "You, Tityrus, lying under the shade of a beech tree..." is the beginning of the Eclogues. So the poet with his artistic sense, has yoked the two books together. He has also poetically given the name of his other work, and the place where he has been writing.

COMMENT: With the end of the fourth Book, it is evident that Virgil is ready to set out on his longed-for task of writing epic. The story goes, however, that the section on Orpheus was written to replace lines praising Gallus, Virgil's one time closest friend. (The tenth Eclogue was addressed to Gallus.) When Gallus fell from the emperor's favor and committed suicide in 26 B.C., Virgil rewrote the final portion of the book. But whatever he may have taken out, Virgil put in lines that perhaps have made the poem even greater.

For in dealing with myth, rather than history, the poet takes his reader from the realm of the particular to the universal. Gallus is dead; most of the world, even in Virgil's time soon forgot him. But the myth of Orpheus and Eurydice, with its eternal truths, lives on forever.

NAMES AND PLACES

MELLA: a river not far from Mantua, flowing into the Po.

CANOPUS: one of the mouths of the Nile, also a city on that mouth. The people were conquered by Alexander of Macedon. The capital of Macedon was Pella, hence the adjective Pellaean.

PERSIANS: here Virgil really means the Parthian bowmen, but Parthian and Persian were more or less interchangeable among the poets.

INDIANS: Virgil means Ethiopians, but the two syllable word in Latin for Indian (Indus) is much easier to put into a line of verse than the four syllable word Aethiopes.

PENEUS: the river-god, father of Cyrene, mother of Aristaeus. (The shepherd's father was the sun-god, Apollo. Virgil invokes Apollo at the beginning of the Book.) The river of this name ran through the valley of Tempe in Thessaly.

THYMBRA: a city in Asia Minor near Troy where there was a famous temple to Apollo.

PHASIS: a river flowing into the eastern end of the Black Sea.

LYCUS: the name of several rivers. Virgil may mean the one in Asia Minor, or he may have them all in mind. The point is that Aristaeus is looking at the sources of all the major rivers.

ENIPEUS: a river in Thessaly flowing into the Peneus.

ANIO: the most famous of the tributaries of the Tiber.

HYPANIS: another river flowing into the Black Sea.

ERIDANUS: a great mythical river, but also another name for the Po.

PANCHAEA: a mythical island near Arabia.

MAEONIA: means Lydia here.

CARPATHIAN SEA: between Rhodes and Crete.

PANGAEUS: a mountain in Macedonia.

RHESUS: a king of Thrace who went to the aid of the Trojans, but was killed before he was able to be of any help.

ORITHYIA: daughter of king Erectheus of Athens. The North wind carried her off to Thrace. Acte was an ancient name for Attica, the section of Greece in which Athens is located.

TAENARUS: a promontory on the southern tip of Greece. Legend said there was a cave there through which Hercules dragged the monster-dog, Cerberus, the guardian of the underworld.

DIS: another name for Pluto, the king of the underworld. The name is also used for the whole of the underworld.

EREBUS: the gloomy place under the earth through which the ghosts of the dead pass.

TARTARUS: the place in the underworld where the wicked were punished.

AVERNUS: a marshy lake in central Italy, thought to be one of the entrances into the underworld.

STRYMON: a river in Macedonia.

TANAIS: now called the Don, in Russia.

OEAGRUS: father of Orpheus, and king of Thrace.

SUMMARY: Virgil writes about the bees in a mock-heroic style. They lead him to the myth-epic of Aristaeus and Orpheus. The second half of the book could exist separately, but the poet has carefully tied it in with his original topic, the bees. Virgil begins the Book by invoking Apollo, and ends with the tale of a son of Apollo. We see also Virgil developing his philosophy, torn between a scientific interpretation of the universe, and the feeling that there are aspects of it which science does not explain. At the end of the book, the poet returns to his adopted hero, Octavius, for this man is the hope of law and order for the world, which becomes the theme of Virgil's greatest work, the Aeneid.

WHAT CRITICS HAVE SAID
ABOUT THE AENEID

Critics have been discussing the Aeneid ever since the days of Virgil himself. It is impossible to include here everything that has been said. Perhaps of greater interest to the modern student is the change in understanding and appreciation of the poet's great work, the Aeneid, which has taken place in the nineteenth and twentieth centuries. In general it can be said that the nineteenth century approach (including the first twenty years or so of the twentieth century also) was one of either condemning Virgil for being inferior to Homer, or one of appreciating him in a sentimental or apologetic way. This criticism, in the words of Viktor Pöschl, the great modern German critic, was "blind to everything artistic", and "the sediment of a rationalism estranged from art and life." (page 5, the Art of Virgil; see list of works below.) On the other side, the modern critic realizes that art, and poetry is most certainly art, must be judged in relation to its own period in history, not in relation to the period in which the critic lives. A poet must be judged by how well he succeeds in the task he set himself, not in how well he succeeds in pleasing the reader. Scholars are now beginning to believe that Virgil must be understood, not so much as an imitator of Homer, but as a critic of Homer. They have given up the centuries old practice of trying to equate Homer and Virgil, or of putting them in the balance and finding one poet lacking.

Below is a list of some of the best known ninteenth and twentieth century scholars in the field, with their works, and their dates. The list includes one French name, Sainte-Beuve, and one German, Viktor Pöschl. There are, of course, many more German scholars of the nineteenth century, but since their labors were mainly to condemn Virgil, they have not been included. Following the list of scholars are the various topics of criticism which most of the authors cover. The topics are illustrated by direct quotes from the works themselves in chronological order of when the books were written. Pöschl's statements usually come last, for he typifies the modern approach. The reader should remember that all the statements represent the subjective appreciation of the various authors. Perhaps it would be a good idea to keep in mind the words of the famous British orator, Edmunde Burke, when he said in his Appeal from the New to the Old Whigs: "We ought not to follow our own fancies, but to study them (the great authors) until we know how and what to admire; and if we cannot arrive at this union of admiration with knowledge, rather to believe that we are dull than that the rest of the world has been imposed on."

CRITICS AND THEIR WORKS

CONINGTON, JOHN. The Works of Virgil: vol. II, George Bell & Sons, London, 1884. 1825-1869.

DUCKWORTH, GEORGE ECKEL. Structural Patterns and Proportions in Virgil's Aeneid. University of Michigan Press, Ann Arbor, 1962.

(The quotes are taken from his article summarizing the book which appeared in Transactions of the American Philological Association, vol. 91, 1960, entitled Mathematical Symmetry in the Aeneid.) 1903- .

DUFF, JOHN WIGHT. A Literary History of Rome — the Golden Age. Charles Scribner's Sons, New York, 1927. 1866-1944.

GLOVER, TERROT REAVELEY. Virgil. Macmillan Co. New York, 1912. 1869-1943.

KNIGHT, W.F. JACKSON. Roman Vergil. Faber & Faber Ltd. London, 1944. 1895- .

MACKAIL, JOHN WILLIAM. Virgil and His Meaning to the World of Today. Marshall Jones & Co. London, 1922. 1859-1945.

NETTLESHIP, HENRY. Suggestions Introductory to a Study of the Aeneid. Clarendon Press, Oxford, 1875.
Vergil. Appleton & Co., New York, 1880. 1839-1893.

PÖSCHL, VIKTOR. (translated by Gerda Seligson) The Art of Vergil. University of Michigan Press, Ann Arbor, 1962. 1910- .

SAINTE-BEUVE, CHARLES AUGUSTIN. Étude sur Virgile. Paris, 1891. 1804-1869.

SELLAR, WILLIAM YOUNG. The Roman Poets of the Augustan Age —Virgil. Clarendon Press, Oxford, 1908. 1825-1890.

A. RELATION TO HOMER

SAINTE-BEUVE: "The first book of the Aeneid is decked with Homer's most famous and conspicuous similes. Virgil displays and presents these at the beginning and in the most obvious places. Far from being embarrassed by this, he takes pride in it." (p. 107) "The immense moral force which emanates from so many of the tableaux of Homer appears more concentrated in Virgil, along with more reflection and in a mirror, so to speak, more clear cut and better defined." (p. 186) "The lesson of taste which one could obtain from it (the first book of the Aeneid) is not to admire Homer or Virgil less, but, as much as possible, to admire each in his own category and age of civilization." (p. 292)

NETTLESHIP: "It can easily be imagined how often this devotion to the Greek epic has spoiled the freshness and spontaneousness of Vergil's writing. But in thus studying and using Homer as no Roman poet had studied and used him before, Vergil thought that he was doing no more than his duty to Latin literature (and he thought that) the never ceasing labour on the great master-piece of Greek literature to be the main condition of success in bringing Latin writing to perfection. --- Vergil's work has suffered by a too rigid adherence to the rules which he had laid down for himself." (Vergil: p. 68)

SELLAR: "He can never again enter into rivalry with Homer as the inspired poet of heroic action." (p. 78) "The interest which he imparts to his narrative is different from, and inferior to, that attaching to the original representation in the Homeric poems. ---Not only was Virgil's own genius much less creative than that of Homer, his materials possessed much less plasticity." (p. 394) "In employment of illustrative imagery Virgil is much more sparing than Homer." (p. 413) "Virgil's instrument fails, or at least is much inferior to Homer's in aptitude for natural dialogue or for bringing familiar things in the freshness of immediate impression before the imagination." (p. 419)

GLOVER: "Virgil has the poet's eye for human life, but he does not see it with Homer's freshness. It is partly because Homer has done or watched the things about which he writes, while Virgil has read about them in books and pictured them with the inner eye." (p. 48) "Virgil falls far short of Homer in expressing the stern joy that warriors feel." (p. 50).

DUFF: "Some inapposite incidents and similes would not have been introduced but for the desire to emulate Homer." (p. 457) "To compensate for the absence of fire, he has exactitude of workmanship and equilibrium of style. ---"Virgil is more critical, urbane, emotional, than Homer." (p. 459) "With greater care for the proprieties there is less nature. Homer keeps the attention more closely, and is more fully believed. What reader can accept the legendary if it is artificially Romanised? ---He has not the imperturbable calm of Homer. ---Virgil is more humane; he is less simply human." (pp. 460-461)

KNIGHT: uses the word "integrates" throughout his book to indicate the relationship of the two poets.

PÖSCHL: "He added depth of feeling and symbolic significance to Homer's direct observations and literal meanings." (p. 3) "This is the central question for both aesthetic criticism and intellectual history, because when one compares Vergil with Homer, one compares---two stages in the history of creative imagination." There is "a strange reenactment of Homer's poetry in the Aeneid and its preservation in the structure of a new work of art." (p. 7) "Vergil's attachment to Homer is akin to Roman reverence for the authority of traditional forms. ---According to the Roman point of view it is possible to create something perfect only by building on to something else which has itself grown slowly in the course of history. One must carry on and repeat past achievements in a new form. ---This exemplifies the peculiar Roman trait of not allowing something once found to be great and true to disappear, but to appeal to it again and again and thus to preserve it." (p. 8) "The crowning achievement of the Roman epic was made possible when for the first time Homer, the representative of Greek art and humanity, was absorbed by an equal. Vergil was Homer's peer in artistic greatness and emotional insight, discrimination, and passion." (p. 9) "The more openly he attests his dependence on Homer, the more ambitiously he strives to surpass him in the perfection of form and interpretation and connection of motifs." (p. 26) "Within the Homeric shell lies the Vergilian kernel." (p. 28) "Loss of natural simplicity is the price paid for perfection of the classical form." (p. 36) Homer is "objective", and Vergil "subjective". (p. 40)

DUCKWORTH: In the central part of the poem "long Homeric episodes (games, trip to underworld, catalogue, description of shield) are reworked for the glorification of Rome and its history, the portrayal of Ancient Italy, and the praise of Augustus and the new Golden Age." (p. 187)

B. POET OF WAR

SELLAR: "In his scenes of battle Virgil is as inferior to Homer as he is in portraying sea adventure. (p. 388)

DUFF: "Virgil does not enjoy the slayings any more than his reader; he is merely overborne by convention." (p. 458)

PÖSCHL: "Rather than banishing Homer's realism from his work, Vergil has toned it down and transfigured it through his art. ---The horrors of war had to be shown—that the strength and glory of Rome might shine all the more." (p. 100) "On the other hand Vergil's scenes (of war) lack the powerful vitality and primitive strength of the Greek epic." (p. 101)

C. CHARACTER OF AENEAS

SELLAR: "---Aeneas is altogether wanting in energy, spontaneity, intellectual resource, and insight." (p. 397) "He undergoes no passionate struggle in resigning Dido." (p. 398) "He is the passive receptacle of Divine guidance." (p. 399)

DUFF: "Dutiful to his old father and to the gods, ---his desertion of Dido--- leaves Aeneas either more or less than human, ---either demigod, or brute. (p. 463) "Aeneas is too often a puppet." (p. 464)

PÖSCHL: Aeneas is the "personification of things Roman" (p. 16); "he realizes the connection of mortal life with world order and that of his own destiny with the history of Rome." (p. 27) "a man of memory and inner vision" (p. 35); he has "compassion for Dido's grief." (p. 44) "He suffers more for the sorrows of others than because of his own misfortune." (p. 44) He is "compassionate." (p. 51) He "prefigures the Christian hero whose heart remains gentle through struggle and sorrow and beats in secret sympathy with all suffering creatures." (p. 53) He "experiences spiritual sorrow to the utmost." (p. 54) He is a man of tragedy because of the "conflict of heroic fulfillment of duty with human sensitivity." (p. 58) His "potentiality for experiencing sorrow grows with the realization of the greatness of his task." (p. 59)

D. SPIRITUAL ELEMENT

SAINTE-BEUVE: "He makes us believe, by the serious sweetness of his words, by the pure light which emanates from his work and his genius, in something polished, brilliant, generally enlightening, in something humane and almost holy." (p. 68) "Virgil, like his hero, has both a quality of piety and pity, occasionally, a touch of sadness, of almost melancholy." (p. 100)

SELLAR: "And though the representation of the outward world in Virgil is, in its serene beauty, suggestive of a secret unceasing life which appeals to the human spirit in its more tranquil moods, yet it does not move the mind to that profounder sense of an affinity between the soul of man and the soul of Nature which the great modern poets awaken." (p. 88) "Virgil produces the most powerful effect by the use of the simplest words in their simplest application. They affect the mind with a strange potency, of which perhaps no account can be given except that they make us feel—the burden of the mystery of life, and by their marvellous beauty, the reflection, it may be, from some light dimly discerned or imagined beyond the gloom, they make it seem more easy to be borne." (p. 423)

MACKAIL: "In none is there so deep a sense of the beauty and sorrow of life, of keen remembrances and shadowy hope, and enfolding all, of infinite pity." (p. 110)

DUFF: "Virgil is spiritual, touched with doctrine, reverie, regrets, misgivings, consecration--. His brooding melancholy he wedded mystically to this strong confidence in the service which his country must render to the world. ---His regard for things of the spirit struck harmonious chords in early Christian hearts--." (p. 462) "Virgil's tender melancholy is merged in his profound reflections. He both thought and felt deeply on life." (p. 469)

PÖSCHL: "Aeneas suffers for the sake of others. A new humanity announc-
ing the Christian philosophy burst forth from him." (p. 53) "Virgil infused
the Roman idea of duty with deep humanity, (bringing) it closer to the Christian
idea of charity and solidarity." (p. 54) He has a "reverence for the mystery
of fate." (p. 73) He believed in "a divine plan controlling and directing universal events." (p. 73) "He emphasizes pain through a reference to joy,
darkness through light, and failure through a final triumph." (p. 172) "Vergil
expresses a religious feeling which precludes the isolation of any one part of
life. ---Every single thing has a place in a divine world where glory and
gloom, reason and emotion, demonic and divine, are restricted and rein-
forced through their opposites." (p. 173)

E. HANDLING OF SIMILES

SELLAR: "Another class of similes---merely give a realistic outward symbol of some movement of the mind or passions without any imaginative en-
hancement of the situation." (p. 414)

PÖSCHL: Homer "aims at illumination of visible relations while Vergil aims
to establish moods, interpret states of mind, and to intimate impending fate.
---Vergilian similes are---more felt than observed." (p. 81) He connected
his similes "most intimately with the interior action which accompanies the
exterior events." (p. 65) "Their function is to give the poem depth---."
(p. 66) "In Vergil's hands the simile is a deeply integrated whole, highlight
and focal point for unfolding events. It is a bold and beautiful picture of the
idea and destiny of epic heroes." (p. 99) "Homer usually concludes his similes with a concrete detail which adds nothing material to what precedes it.
Vergil concludes his similes with an image that satisfies the musical require-
ment for a beautiful chord." (p. 161)

F. CENTRAL IDEA OF POEM

SAINTE-BEUVE: In the Aeneid we see that "triumph is always incomplete,
unachieved, and mixed with shadow; these are the miseries of even victory,
the sad resemblance and almost equality of the conquerors and the con-
quered---." (p. 186)

NETTLESHIP: "The primary purpose of the Aeneid---is---not so much to
delineate 'character' as to exhibit the conflict of forces." (Suggestions: p. 36)
"The Aeneid is therefore a poem of which the main idea is Roman, the mythology a bastard mixture of Greek and Italian, and the arrangement and handling
wholly Greek." (Vergil: p. 61)

DUFF: "His central idea is to uphold the new monarchy as one foreshadowed
in the fatherly leadership of Aeneas, and predestined to follow the long and
glorious evolution of the republic. It is a historic idea majestic in its historic
associations. It flattered the national pride, but it did not stir the heart."(p. 465)

PÖSCHL: The basic theme of the poem is "the struggle and final victory of
order. ---The demonic appears in history as civil or foreign war, in the soul
as passion, and in nature as death and destruction. Jupiter, Aeneas, and

Augustus are its conquerors, while Juno, Dido, Turnus, and Antony are its conquered representatives." (p. 18) "The Aeneid is a poem of humanity, not a political manifesto. In it, myth and history acquire meaning and grandeur as expression of a higher level, the realization of a divine order, the symbol of the cosmic law of destiny revealed in the existence of the world of man." (p. 23)

DUCKWORTH: "The epic rises far above the patriotic and historical level in the poet's dramatic treatment of character and event, and in his introduction of loftier themes of philosophy and religion; it is an epic not only of Rome but of human life as well." (p. 185) "The Aeneid is the story of Aeneas but it is also the story of the destiny of Rome under Augustus. This latter provides much of the central core of the poem (V-VIII) and concludes with the victories and triumphs of Augustus as described on the shield at the end of VIII." (p. 186)

G. ART AND STYLE

SAINTE-BEUVE: "Virgil, from the hour when he appeared has been the poet of Latinity in its entirety. He gave a new form to taste, to passion, and to sensitivity." (p. 1) "When a poet has the talent and the artistic skill to express thus the present and actual feelings of his nation, to exalt the feeling of its dominion and its triumph, and also to reflect and paint distant horizons and incredibilities of remotest times, and unites all these, he does not fail to delight, and to elevate his century for posterity." (p. 79)

CONINGTON: " In undertaking the Aeneid at the command of a superior, Virgil was venturing beyond the province of his genius." (Introduction to vol. II. page xix.)

NETTLESHIP: " ---Vergil was able by his wonderful power of style to produce work which marks the climax of a particular kind of poetry, which completes and embodies in itself much that preceding poets had been striving after, and which gave the law to succeeding generations of writers." (Vergil: p. 1) "His genius was fitted more for the elaboration of detail than for the clear grasping of general conceptions." (Vergil: p. 98)

SELLAR: " The Aeneid as an epic poem representative of the Roman Empire --does not touch the heart or enlighten the conscience: and this is an important drawback to the claim which the Aeneid may have to the highest rank as a work of art." (p. 354) "In the Aeneid Virgil's style appears as great in its power of reaching the secrets of the human spirit as in the Georgics it proved itself to be in eliciting the deeper meaning of Nature." (p. 421)

DUFF: " To compensate for the absence of fire he has exactitude of workmanship and equilibrium of style." (p. 459) "Words are combined with theme so that the Virgilian musings, descriptions, speeches, rich in a compassionate tenderness, attain the finished beauty of a solemn music." (p. 470) "The beauty of Virgil's style was produced by a minute and sedulous shaping of words in the endeavor to satisfy the imperious demands of a refined self-criticism and an ear divinely attuned---Virgil's ideal was the choice of words which in themselves and in association are winsome, impressive, and worthy of a noble theme." (p. 477) " Under Virgil's verbal sorcery, Latin becomes a golden language of exquisite richness, veined with a delicate melancholy, and wistful reverie upon the abundant travail of life. " (p. 478)

KNIGHT: " There is layer on layer of thought and emotion, coinciding marvel- lously in the end. The chief layers are the forms and contents of Greek poems —current thought and feeling and symbolism of Vergil's own time—the Roman tradition of history guided by destiny, and the historical or legendary condi- tions and events of the Mediterranean world at the end of the age of bronze, and of Italy in the earlier centuries of Rome. " (p. 100)

PÖSCHL: " One of the most important principles of Vergil's art (is) the striv- ing for unity. "   (p. 31) The " preference for 'grandeur,' 'pathos,' and the 'sublime' is a marked characteristic of Vergil's style. "   (p. 142)   " With consummate artistry, Vergil has made ---landscape fit the mood and charac- ter of---action. " (p. 142) "Since Vergil, 'mood' has become to poetry what 'light' is to painting---Vergil's poem is a stream of moods and feelings blended delicately together and which move the heart with melody and lead from one emotional quality to another. " (p. 156) "---sequence of mood---is the core of the narrative.   Viewed as a whole, it proceeds in a swelling and ebbing motion or in recurring waves. " (p. 157) "Throughout the poem there is a rhythmic pattern of light and shadow. " (p. 165) "Vergil's aesthetic con- cept, like all Classical concepts, postulates the harmonious balance of oppo- sites. " (p. 173)

DUCKWORTH: There are three structural patterns: " l) the alternation of the books, those with even numbers being of a more serious and tragic nature than those with odd numbers which are lighter and serve to relieve the tension; 2) parallelism by similarity and contrast between books in each half, I and VII, II and VIII etc.; 3) a tripartite division of the epic into three groups of four books each---It is thus a trilogy with the first four books the tragedy of Dido, and the last four books the tragedy of Turnus, enclosing in a framework pat- tern the central portion, where long Homeric episodes---are reworked---for the glorification of Rome---and the praise of Augustus and the new Golden Age. " (pp. 186 ff.) He goes on to say that the individual books within the poem are based on tripartite divisions of major and minor episodes.   The number of lines in the major and minor passages can be shown to have a mathematical ratio of approximately .618. This was the number known to the ancients as the Golden Section, or the Golden Mean. If we let m equal the number of lines in the minor episode, and $\underline{M}$ equal the number of lines in the Major episode, we would have the following statement:

$$\frac{m}{M} \quad as \quad \frac{M}{m+M}$$

An example would be a group of lines in book III. The shorter passage is from line 1-191 (m=191); the longer is 192-505 (M=310.8 because there are some incomplete lines and he rounds these to a per cent $=\frac{310.8}{501.8}= .6185.$ (pp. 192-198; he goes into considerably more detail than this.) This suggests that Vergil wishes the listener to be conscious of the mathematical symmetry of the poem or to derive a subconscious pleasure from the harmony of the proportions. " (p. 201)

H. ORIGINALITY

NETTLESHIP: "His imitations seem crude, obvious, often inappropriate."
Suggestions: p. 27) "The Roman poets were still simple enough to think that
open imitation was rather a grace than a defect." (Suggestions: p. 29)

SELLAR: "Virgil's power as an epic poet does not consist in original inven-
tion of incident or action, but in combining diverse elements into a homogeneous
whole, and imparting poetic life to old materials, many of them not originally
conceived in a poetic spirit." (p. 394)

DUFF: "The originality of Virgil is most manifest where he is most natural. "
(p. 461) "To minimize his creative gifts — either on the ground of his borrow-
ing of conventions, as if he were a second-hand plagiarist, or on the ground of
his conscious aim, as if he overdid the didactic — is to miss the significance
of Virgil's relation to his age." (p. 482)

KNIGHT: "The success of Vergil is partly due to his willed or spontaneous,
perhaps unconscious patience — in waiting till the wealth of his thought and
feeling and observation, much of it directly taken from the contemporary world,
gathered sufficient literary and traditional material to frame or mould or con-
strain, and so make artistic and universal, all that his keen artistic and practical
vigilance had acquired." (p. 145)

PÖSCHL: "In Vergil's poetry everything participates in the inner drama and
reflects the poet's awareness of the stirrings within the souls of his characters and of the destiny inherent in the events. Everything—landscape, morning,
evening—movement and image becomes a symbol of the soul. The cadence of
each line radiates an inner light and shimmers with nuances of feeling---It is
easily seen how much of what was inexpressible before is now within the range
of expression and how great a debt later poets owe Vergil. In this light it
seems more than foolish to doubt Vergil's 'originality.' Such doubt arises
from a profound misunderstanding of Vergil's poetry and of artistic creativity
in general." (p. 3) "His critics and his apologists, influenced by the obvious
borrowings, overlooked the decisive changes beneath the surface. This may
serve as a warning against the type of interpretation which almost always
tacitly assumes that Vergil simply appropriated the content of older works
along with the motifs, be it in relation to Homer—or Naevius and Ennius. He
did not do that! The secret of his originality is hidden in the transformation,
connection, and deepening of the motifs to which he gave another meaning and
a new beauty. He did this through sensitive changes, through a web of myste-
rious references, through novel light and sound effects. Such artistry with line
and color, composition and combination, is the very nature of his poetry. In
a word, it is the form through which a new soul emerges as if by magic from
the borrowed material. An inner readiness, a loving, if critical contemplation,
is needed to recognize it." (p. 68)

SAMPLE QUESTIONS AND ANSWERS

1. Why read Virgil?

There are many answers to this question, but one of the most important is that he, more than any other poet, established the ascendency of Roman culture (and thus Greek culture because the Roman incorporated the Greek) and ideas in the history of Western thought. The Aeneid was a "classic" as soon as it was published, and Virgil's influence grew greater rather than diminished in succeeding generations. He was one of the few classic authors well known throughout the period of the "Dark" and "Middle" ages. This was due primarily to the tremendous spiritual side of his poetry and the sonorous music of the lines. A knowledge of Virgil's poetry deepens immeasurably our ability to appreciate the great poets of the Renaissance, such as Dante, Dryden, Milton, or Shakespeare. His work can truly be considered, in Pöschl's words: "one of the bibles of the Western world." (The Art of Virgil: p. 12).

2. What do Virgil's works reveal about his philosophy?

Virgil was a deep thinker. Even his earliest works show this. But his ideas changed somewhat as he grew older. In his youth he was more of an idealist. To a certain degree, he really believed in the possibility of a Golden Age as the exalted tones of the fourth Eclogue show. He was influenced by the Epicurean idea of science as the explanation for the universe, of tranquility through knowledge, and of the steady progress of mankind. These ideas appear most strongly in the Georgics. At the same time the Georgics have a certain Stoic element as well as Epicurean, with their emphasis on duty and hard work, and a suggestion of a divine spirit permeating the universe. The Georgics also contain many traces of Virgil's more youthful belief in and longing for the Golden Age. But in this later work he is much less certain that it will come. The Golden Age is an ideal in the Georgics. In the Eclogues it is a possible reality.

The Aeneid is the great proponent of Stoic doctrine. It stresses respect for character, belief in divine ordering of the world, a sense of duty, and inner strength which gives control over fortune. It also emphasizes the concept of a unity of the cosmos and the state. But Virgil was more than an adherent to a particular brand of philosophy. Like any man searching for spiritual truths, he held to some concepts and rejected others. The Epicurean explanation of atoms and void combining to create everything in the universe did not satisfy answers to questions about love, endurance, or that greatest of all Roman virtues, pietas (loving and willing performance of one's duty to ancestors, parents, the gods and the state). Virgil believed in a universe divinely created and controlled according to laws, both physical and moral. But he did not define the degree to which free will and divine guidance can exist side by side. A spiritual element exists in all of Virgil's works, and ultimately every person who reads with a searching mind will find something relevant to his own outlook on life.

3. What are the subjects of the Eclogues?

The Eclogues have really no one theme. Rather they are a group of individual poems with different subjects such as the beauty of the Italian countryside, the need for friends, and sensitivity to the wrongs done to these friends, admiration for important statesmen, celebration of important contemporary events, the longing for the Golden Age, and the feelings of the heart.

4. What are the main themes of the Georgics?

The great idea of the poem is the importance of peace, both spiritual and physical. There are two ways to achieve this peace. One is through willing and cheerful hard work. The other is by understanding one's own place in the universe. The early Greek poet, Hesiod, is the model for much of the first; the Roman Epicurean poet, Lucretius, is the model for much of the second. But Virgil goes beyond the purely didactic or purely scientific approach. In uniting the physical drudge of labor with the spiritual satisfaction of a job well done, and the scientific aspects of nature with his own appreciation for natural beauty, he creates a poem which continually inspires his readers.

5. What are the major themes of the Aeneid?

First and foremost, the Aeneid is a poem symbolizing Rome's destiny. Virgil had a passionate conviction in the greatness of Rome. The belief was not implanted in him by order from Augustus. It came from within his own soul. This greatness, which Virgil believed came to pass because of the joining of high ideals with primitive strength, was manifest in the past in the struggle with the Italian tribes (which covered many generations of Roman history) and later with Carthage. The struggle with Carthage is symbolized in Book IV where Aeneas is finally victorious over his feelings for Dido. The struggle with the Italian tribes is symbolized in the hero's final conquering of Turnus. These are examples of the great theme: the struggle and final victory of order. There is also the theme of the symbolic relationship between nature and politics, myth and history. This included the concept that Roman order was founded in the divine whole; pietas was its greatest virtue. A third theme is the idea of tragedy — the tragedy of human life and Roman history because of the conflict between duty and desire. Yet in spite of the awareness of tragedy, the Aeneid is a poem of hope, hope that order will conquer chaos, and that out of suffering will come peace and joy.

6. What is the purpose of Virgil's similes?

The main purpose of Virgil's similes is to create mood and atmosphere, and show how the characters feel. They establish not so much a visual picture as a mental image of a person's state of mind. They also serve to suggest impending fate. For these reasons they add not just a pictorial quality but a spiritual depth to the poem.

7. What is the role of the gods in the Aeneid?

The gods play a double role. They are connected directly with the action in the plot, partly from the epic convention of having the gods take part in the story, but more important, as illustrating the idea that there is a divine plan controlling history. Every historical event has two levels: one is the human level with its desires and intentions; the other is the divine, which manipulates these events. The second role of the gods is to symbolize the various aspects of human character. Jupiter, the king of the gods, is a symbol of man's ability to organize and control himself both mentally and physically. Juno, the queen of the gods, is a symbol of the opposite elements, such as anger, which causes a person to lose control of himself and the situation. Jupiter has power (potestas) because he has control. The role of Venus, the goddess of love, is one of a protectress and a calm, reassuring influence; not of exciting to passion, strange as this may seem. This is basically because she is the mother of Aeneas. Her importance in the story is due to her motherhood, not her divinity. Thus the divine and human are interwoven throughout the poem, with Jupiter as the ruler of both.

8. Why are there two ways of spelling Virgil's name?

The poet's name is spelt with an e in all the early imperial inscriptions and in the earliest and best manuscripts of his works. There is evidence that there was a certain amount of fluctuation in spelling during the last century of the Republic, but the poet refers to himself as Vergilius. Possibly due to the change in pronunciation, his name came to be commonly spelt with an i by the fifth century A.D. This spelling continued during the Middle Ages and the Renaissance. It was also the general spelling in the nineteenth century. Recently, however, scholars are trying to go back to the Ver spelling since it is recognized as the correct one from the manuscripts.

BIBLIOGRAPHY AND
GUIDE TO FURTHER RESEARCH

Bailey, Cyril. Religion in Virgil. Clarendon Press, Oxford, 1935.

Comparetti, Domenico (trans. by E. F. M. Benecke). Virgil in the Middle Ages. the Macmillan Co. , New York, 1908.

Connington, John and Nettleship, Henry. The Works of Virgil (2 vols.) George Bell and Sons, London; 1858. 1884.

Duckworth, George Eckel. Structural Patterns and Proportions in Vergil's Aeneid. University of Michigan Press, Ann Arbor, 1962.

Frank, Tenney. Vergil, a Biography. Clarendon Press, Oxford, 1922.

Glover, T. R. Virgil. the Macmillan Co. , New York, 1912.

*Highet, Gilbert. Poets in a Landscape. Alfred A. Knopf, New York, 1957.

Knight, W. F. Jackson. Roman Virgil. Faber & Faber, Ltd. , London, 1953.

Letters, F. J. H. Virgil. Sheed & Ward, New York, 1946.

Mackail, J. W. Virgil and his Meaning to the World of Today. Marshall Jones Co. , Boston, 1922.

Nettleship, Henry. Suggestions Introductory to a Study of the Aeneid. Clarendon Press, Oxford, 1875.
Vergil. Appleton & Co., New York, 1880.

Nitchie, Elizabeth. Vergil and the English Poets. Columbia University Press, New York City, 1919.

Oxford Classical Dictionary. Clarendon Press, Oxford; 1957.

*Pöschl, Victor (trans. by Gerta Seligson). The Art of Vergil. University of Michigan Press, Ann Arbor, 1962.

Prescott, Henry W. The Development of Virgil's Art. University of Chicago Press, Chicago, 1927.

*Rand, Edward Kennard. The Magical Art of Virgil. Harvard University Press, Cambridge, 1931.

Sellar, William Young. The Roman Poets of the Augustan Age — Virgil. Clarendon Press, Oxford, 1908.

Smith, William and Anthon, Charles. A New Classical Dictionary. Harper Bros. , New York, 1851.

Syme, Ronald. The Roman Revolution. Clarendon Press, Oxford, 1939.

* especially useful

NOTES

NOTES

NOTES

NOTES

NOTES

NOTES

MONARCH® NOTES AND STUDY GUIDES

ARE AVAILABLE AT RETAIL STORES EVERYWHERE

In the event your local bookseller cannot provide you with other Monarch titles you want —

ORDER ON THE FORM BELOW:

Complete order form appears on inside front & back covers for your convenience.

Simply send retail price, local sales tax, if any, plus 35¢ per book to cover mailing and handling.

TITLE #	AUTHOR & TITLE (exactly as shown on title listing)	PRICE
	PLUS ADDITIONAL 35¢ PER BOOK FOR POSTAGE	
	GRAND TOTAL	$

MONARCH® PRESS, a Simon & Schuster Division of Gulf & Western Corporation
Mail Service Department, 1230 Avenue of the Americas, New York, N.Y. 10020

I enclose $ .... to cover retail price, local sales tax, plus mailing and handling.

Name _____
(Please print)
Address _____

City _____ State _____ Zip _____

Please send check or money order. We cannot be responsible for cash.